D0871449

ORSON SCOTT CARD

FORMIC WARS

BURNING EARTH

ORSON SCOTT CARD
FORMIC WARS

Creative Director & Executive Director:
ORSON SCOTT CARD
Plot: **ORSON SCOTT CARD & AARON JOHNSTON**
Script: **AARON JOHNSTON**
Art: **GIANCARLO CARACUZZO**

Color Art: **JIM CHARALAMPIDIS**
Letterer: **CORY PETIT**
Cover Art: **SALVADOR LARROCA & ARON LUSEN; JENNY FRISON; AND BILLY TAN & GURU EFX**

Editor: **JORDAN D. WHITE**
Senior Editor: **NICK LOWE**

Special thanks to
KRISTINE CARD, KATHLEEN BELLAMY, DARIAN ROBBINS, ANDREW BAUGHAN, RALPH MACCHIO, LAUREN SANKOVITCH, JIM NAUSEDAS,JIM MCCANN, ARUNE SINGH & JEFF SUTER

Collection Editor: **JENNIFER GRÜNWALD**
Editorial Assistants: **JAMES EMMETT & JOE HOCHSTEIN**
Assistant Editors: **ALEX STARBUCK & NELSON RIBEIRO**
Editor, Special Projects:
MARK D. BEAZLEY
Senior Editor, Special Projects:
JEFF YOUNGQUIST
Vice President of Creative: **TOM MARVELLI**
Senior Vice President of Sales:
DAVID GABRIEL
Senior Vice President of Strategic Development: **RUWAN JAYATILLEKE**
SVP of Brand Planning & Communications:
MICHAEL PASCIULLO
Book Designer: **RODOLFO MURAGUCHI**

Editor in Chief: **AXEL ALONSO**
Chief Creative Officer: **JOE QUESADA**
Publisher: **DAN BUCKLEY**

ENDER'S GAME: FORMIC WARS — BURNING EARTH. Contains material originally published in magazine form as FORMIC WARS: BURNING EARTH #1-7. First printing 2011. ISBN# 978-0-7851-3609-5. Published by MARVEL WORLDWIDE, INC., a subsidiary of MARVEL ENTERTAINMENT, LLC. OFFICE OF PUBLICATION: 135 West 50th Street, New York, NY 10020. **Printed in the U.S.A**. ALAN FINE, EVP - Office of the President, Marvel Worldwide, Inc. and EVP & CMO Marvel Characters B.V.; DAN BUCKLEY, Publisher & President - Print, Animation & Digital Divisions; JOE QUESADA, Chief Creative Officer; JIM SOKOLOWSKI, Chief Operating Officer; DAVID BOGART, SVP of Business Affairs & Talent Management; TOM BREVOORT, SVP of Publishing; C.B. CEBULSKI, SVP of Creator & Content Development; DAVID GABRIEL, SVP of Publishing Sales & Circulation; MICHAEL PASCIULLO, SVP of Brand Planning & Communications; JIM O'KEEFE, VP of Operations & Logistics; DAN CARR, Executive Director of Publishing Technology; SUSAN CRESPI, Editorial Operations Manager; ALEX MORALES, Publishing Operations Manager; STAN LEE, Chairman Emeritus. For information regarding advertising in Marvel Comics or on Marvel.com, please contact John Dokes, SVP Integrated Sales and Marketing, at jdokes@marvel.com. For Marvel subscription inquiries, please call 800-217-9158. **Manufactured between 7/25/2011 and 8/22/2011 by R.R. DONNELLEY, INC., SALEM, VA, USA.**

10 9 8 7 6 5 4 3 2 1

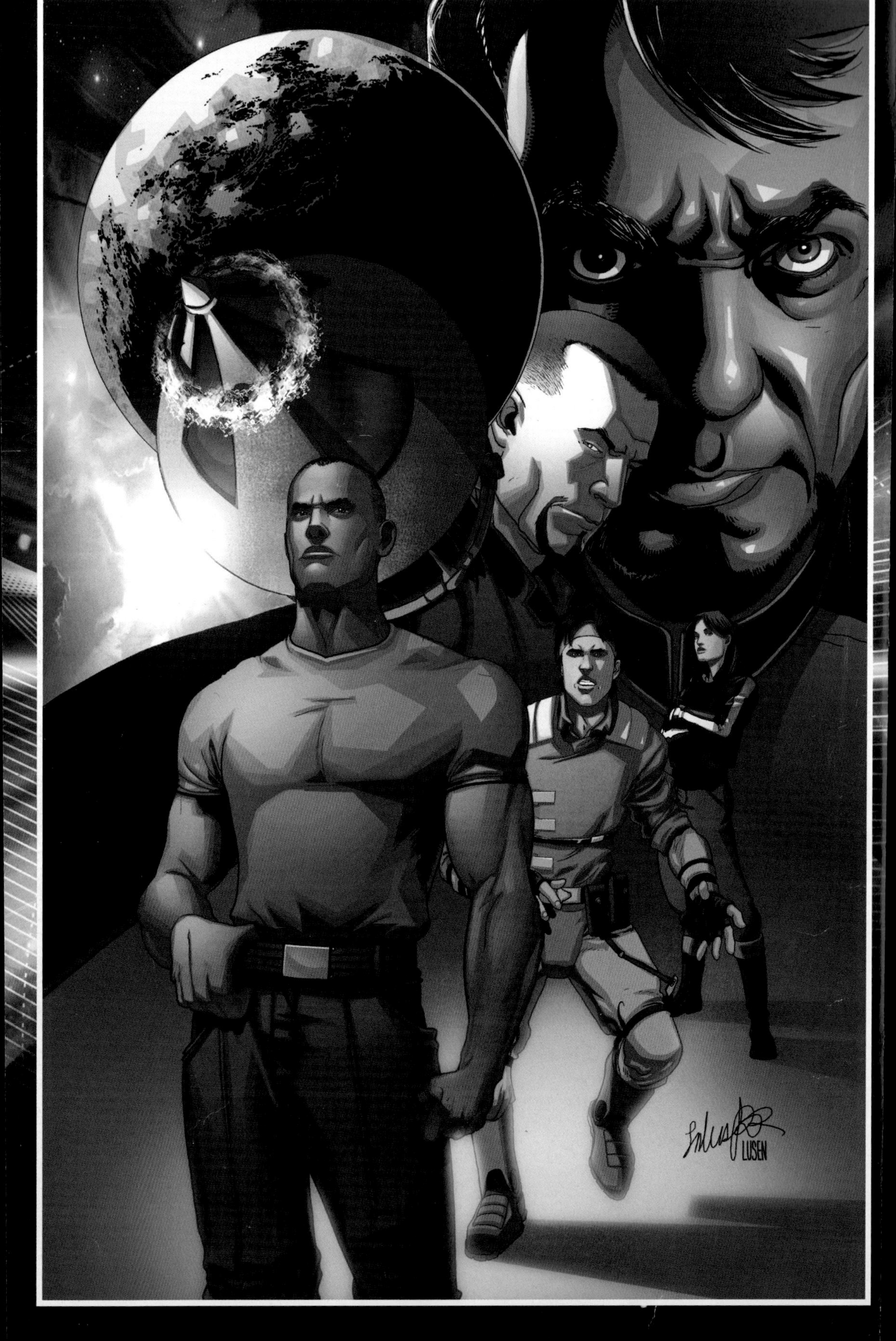

O N E

"History is normally written about those who want to be remembered: politicians and generals and heads of state—people who seek positions of power, not only to make an impact on the world, but also to be glorified by it.

"An accurate history of the First Formic War, however, must place less emphasis on dignitaries and a greater emphasis on what society would call 'normal' individuals. This was not a war won by large-scale military maneuvering, political concessions or carefully crafted treaties. This was a war won by courage and tenacity and improvisational warfare on a very small scale. This was a war won by asteroid miners and accountants, parents and grandparents, soldiers and armed citizens, everyday men and women who put aside their fears and did extraordinary things, not in the interest of self-preservation, but to preserve the human race."

- A History of the Formic Wars, Volume One, Demosthenes

THE KUIPER BELT.
CORPORATE MINING VESSEL, A-CLASS.
PROPERTY OF JUKE LIMITED.
JUKE LTD 45-BX
I GOT CHATTER, LEM.
SOUNDS LIKE, I DON'T KNOW, PORTUGUESE, MAYBE?
GIVE ME YOUR HEADPHONES.
THAT'S SPANISH, GENIUS.
SPANISH, PORTUGUESE. SAME DIFFERENCE.
TRACK THAT FREQUENCY. I WANT TO KNOW EXACTLY WHERE IT'S COMING FROM.
IS IT A FAMILY, LEM? IS IT FREE MINERS?
WE'RE IN THE KUIPER BELT, CHUBS. WHO ELSE WOULD IT BE? PONCE DE LEON?
PONTS DE LA WHAT?

FREQUENCY'S REGISTERED TO A FAMILY FROM VENEZUELA. THE SHIP'S CALLED EL CAVADOR.
HOW BIG IS IT?
SMALL. D CLASS. OLD, TOO. WE COULD BUMP THEM EASILY.
JUKE
JUKE
BUMP THEM? YOU MEAN KNOCK THEM OFF THEIR DIG SITE?
IS THAT FAIR?
NO OFFENSE, BUT I'D RATHER NOT HAVE TO TELL MY FATHER THAT WE DIDN'T MAKE QUOTA BECAUSE, GOSH, IT JUST WOULDN'T HAVE BEEN FAIR.
THIS ISN'T THE ASTEROID BELT. ROCKS OUT HERE WITH GOOD MINERALS ARE FEW AND FAR BETWEEN.
WHEN WE FIND ONE, WE TAKE IT.
BESIDES--
--I'M BORED.

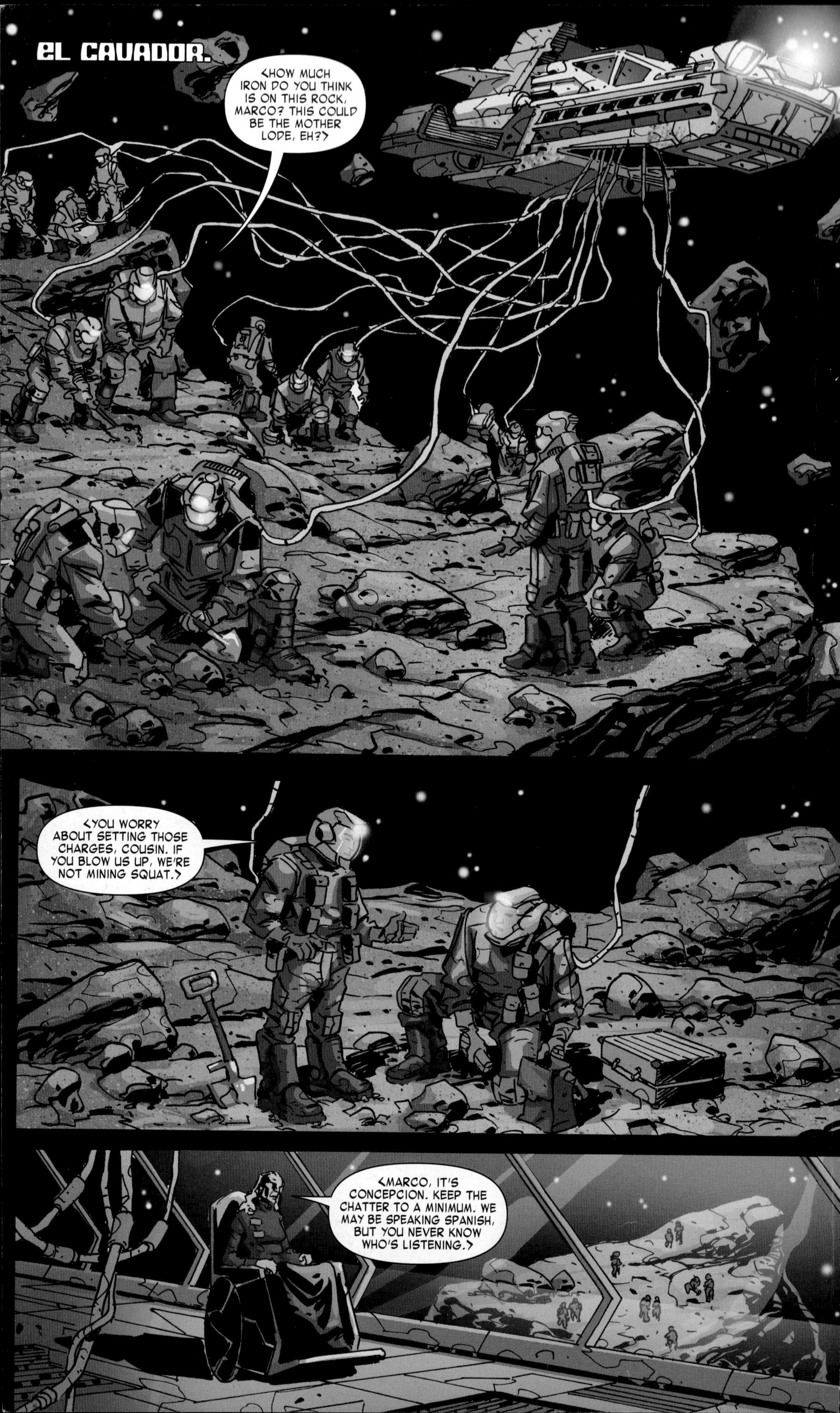
EL CAVADOR.
<HOW MUCH IRON DO YOU THINK IS ON THIS ROCK, MARCO? THIS COULD BE THE MOTHER LODE, EH?>
<YOU WORRY ABOUT SETTING THOSE CHARGES, COUSIN. IF YOU BLOW US UP, WE'RE NOT MINING SQUAT.>
<MARCO, IT'S CONCEPCION. KEEP THE CHATTER TO A MINIMUM. WE MAY BE SPEAKING SPANISH, BUT YOU NEVER KNOW WHO'S LISTENING.>

<AND TRIPLE-CHECK THOSE EXPLOSIVES.>
<IF WE DON'T PLACE AN EQUAL AMOUNT ON BOTH SIDES OF THE ROCK, WE COULD KNOCK IT OUT OF ORBIT AND SEND IT HURTLING AWAY, POSSIBLY EVEN TO EARTH.>
<AT LEAST IT WOULD *SEE* EARTH. THAT'S MORE THAN I CAN SAY.>
<*DIG US A LOAD, MARCO, AND WE'LL BUY OURSELVES A SMALL ISLAND.*>
<SANDY BEACHES?>
<AND ALL THE MALTA YOU CAN DRINK.>
<KEEP SAYING IT, CONCEPCION. ONE DAY I MIGHT BELIEVE IT.>
<TELL VICTOR TO HAVE THOSE NETS UP. WE'RE ALMOST SET TO DETONATE.>
C1

WORKSHOP. EL CAVADOR.
<DON'T LOOK AT THE LIGHT, MONO. IT'LL HURT YOUR EYES.>
<WHAT'S THAT THING YOU'RE FIXING, VICTOR? IS THAT PART OF THE NETS? HOW LONG WILL IT TAKE TO FIX IT? MY DAD SAYS YOU CAN FIX ANYTHING. CAN YOU FIX A CORPORATE SHIP TOO? I BET YOU COULD.>
<NOW WHY WOULD I FIX A CORPORATE, MONO? IF YOU DO A BULLY A FAVOR, HE'LL ONLY PUNCH YOU IN THE GUT.>
<HAVE YOU EVER BEEN PUNCHED IN THE GUT BEFORE? I BET YOU HAVE. I BET IT DIDN'T HURT YOU ONE BIT, DID IT, HUH, VICTOR?>
<THIS METAL'S CRAP. I NEED A NEW PIECE.>
<WHY DON'T YOU JUST GET A NEW PART?>
<LET ME GIVE YOU A LESSON IN ECONOMICS, MONO. WE CAN'T AFFORD SPARE PARTS. WE MAKE DO WITH WHAT WE'VE GOT.>
<AND BELIEVE ME, THAT AIN'T MUCH.>

<I BET THE CORPORATE SHIPS HAVE ALL KINDS OF SPARE PARTS.>
<PROBABLY.>
<AND DIGGERS. AND MOVERS. AND ENGINEERS. AND MECHANICS.>
<YEAH, BUT THEY DON'T HAVE YOU. YOU'RE WORTH MORE THAN A MILLION OF THEIR MECHANICS.>
<DON'T YOU DARE TAKE ANOTHER OF MY COOKIE SHEETS, VICTOR.>
<SORRY, LIZBET. IT'S THAT OR NO NETS.>
<THERE. SEE? GOOD AS NEW.>
<WE JUST WON'T BE EATING AS MANY COOKIES IN THE FUTURE.>
<NOW LET'S SEE IF IT ACTUALLY WORKS.>

<MARCO, IT'S CONCEPCION. THE NETS ARE UP AND READY. REPEAT, VICTOR'S GOT THE NETS UP. WE ARE READY TO DETONATE. OVER.>
<ROGER THAT. THIS FIRST BLAST WILL PROBABLY ONLY BREAK LOOSE A LOT OF SURFACE ROCK, BUT MAYBE WE'LL GET LUCKY.>
<BLAST SITE CLEAR?>
<CHECK. EVERYONE'S ON BOARD BUT YOU.>
<THEN PREPARE FOR DETONATION.>
<AND FOR THE SAKE OF OUR RUMBLING STOMACHS, LET'S HOPE WE STRIKE SOME IRON.>
?
<OH NO.>

JUKE LTD 45-BX
<PARDON THE INTERRUPTION, CAVADOR. BUT THIS SITE IS BETTER SUITED FOR THOSE PROPERLY EQUIPPED FOR THE JOB.>
<SHOULD YOU FEEL THIS AN INCONVENIENCE, PLEASE FORWARD ALL COMPLAINTS TO JUKE LIMITED DOT NET BACKSLASH NOBODY CARES.>

<MARCO!>
<HE'S NOT RESPONDING. VICTOR, PULL HIM IN! PULL HIM IN NOW!>
<HE'S NOT BREATHING.>
<PUT HIM DOWN GENTLY. GET HIS HELMET OFF.>
<HIS NECK. IT'S--BROKEN.>
<NO. NOT MARCO.>
<SOMEONE DO SOMETHING. CONCEPCION, PLEASE.>
<I'M SORRY, LIZBET.>
<MARCO, MY SON. MY HEAVEN. MY LIFE.>

FOUR HOURS LATER.
<ONE OF THE COMPRESSORS IS SHOT AND THE EVAPORATOR IS CRUSHED. IT'S GOING TO GET COLD IN HERE REAL QUICK IF I DON'T FIX THEM.>
<WHAT ABOUT THE CORPORATES?>
<SO YOU CAN FIX THEM?>
<ANSWER THE QUESTION, VICTOR. CAN YOU FIX THEM OR NOT?>
<I CAN JURY-RIG SOMETHING, BUT I DOUBT IT'LL LAST FOR MORE THAN A FEW MONTHS.>
<THEN DO IT.>
<BUT FIRST HACK JUKE LIMITED AND TELL ME WHO CAPTAINS THAT SHIP.>
<IT'S LEM JUKES.>
<UKKO JUKES'S SON?>
<WHAT'S THE ENGLISH EXPRESSION, THE APPLE DOESN'T FALL FAR FROM THE TREE?>
<FIND THEIR FREQUENCY.>

LEM, THE CAVADOR IS HAILING US. THEY'RE ASKING FOR *YOU.*
LEM JUKES AT YOUR SERVICE. YOU KNOW, YOU VENEZUELANS SHOULD REALLY WATCH YOUR DRIVING. THAT COULD HAVE BEEN A NASTY COLLISION.
YOU KILLED A MAN. I DOUBT YOU CARE. I DOUBT YOU'LL LOSE A MINUTE OF SLEEP OVER THAT FACT, BUT I WANTED YOU TO KNOW THAT YOU TOOK AN INNOCENT LIFE.
I--I DIDN'T KNOW. THAT WASN'T MY INTENT.

NO? THEN WHAT WAS YOUR INTENT? TO FRIGHTEN US? TO SHOW OFF?
YOUR FATHER WOULD BE REAL PROUD, LEM. YOU'RE JUST LIKE HIM.

SHAKK!

SHEESH, LEM, WHAT DID THEY SAY?

THE MOON.
CORPORATE HEADQUARTERS OF JUKE LIMITED.
LADIES AND GENTLEMEN, ESTEEMED GUESTS, MEMBERS OF THE PRESS, PLEASE GIVE A WARM WELCOME TO THE PRESIDENT AND CEO OF JUKE LIMITED--
JUKE LIMITED
--MR. UKKO JUKES.
THANK YOU.
TODAY IS A SPECIAL DAY IN THE HISTORY OF THIS ORGANIZATION.
FOR THE PAST TWENTY-FIVE YEARS, JUKE LIMITED HAS BEEN THE LEADER IN SPACE MINING, EXTRACTING HUNDREDS OF MILLIONS OF TONS OF MINERALS A YEAR.
GENERATING TRILLIONS OF DOLLARS FOR THE ECONOMIES OF THE WORLD.
I WONDER HOW MUCH OF THAT IS DIRTY MONEY?
QUIET, IMALA. NOT NOW.

BUT TODAY, THE SPACE MINING INDUSTRY IS TAKING A REVOLUTIONARY STEP FORWARD.
TODAY WE ARE UNVEILING A NEW TECHNOLOGY THAT WILL DRASTICALLY IMPROVE OUR OPERATIONAL EFFICIENCIES.
TODAY, LADIES AND GENTLEMEN, I GIVE YOU--
THE VANGUARD.
THE WORLD'S FIRST SPACE MINING DRONE.
WORKING AS A SCOUT, THE VANGUARD WILL SEEK OUT MINERAL-RICH ASTEROIDS THROUGHOUT THE SOLAR SYSTEM, SIGNIFICANTLY REDUCING TIME MINERS SPEND PROSPECTING.
SHARES OF JUKE LIMITED SURGED FOLLOWING THE ANNOUNCEMENT.
Planet network
CEO UKKO JUKES BRUSHED ASIDE QUESTIONS OF CORPORATE IMPROPRIETY IN CONNECTION WITH THE RECENT ANTITRUST LAWSUIT INITIATED AND THEN DROPPED BY THE GLOBAL TRADE COMMISSION.

OFFICES OF THE LUNAR TRADE DEPARTMENT.
YOU'RE TELLING ME THAT JUKE LIMITED LAUNDERED EIGHTY BILLION DOLLARS LAST YEAR?
JUST LOOK AT THE NUMBERS, FAREED. PLEASE. TEN MINUTES. THAT'S ALL I ASK.
IMALA, I LIKE YOU. YOU'RE SMART. YOU HAVE A WAY WITH NUMBERS. EVERYONE SEES THAT.
BUT YOU'RE ALSO INCREDIBLY INEXPERIENCED.
THAT'S A NICE WAY OF SAYING NAIVE.
HOW LONG HAVE YOU BEEN IN FINANCIAL OVERSIGHT? THREE MONTHS?
SEVEN.
SOME OF THE PEOPLE ON YOUR TEAM HAVE TWENTY YEARS IN THIS, IMALA. TWENTY. YEARS.
YOU'RE TELLING ME THAT YOU SEE HOLES IN THE ACCOUNTING THAT THEY DON'T? GAPING, GLARINGLY OBVIOUSLY HOLES?
DO YOU HAVE ANY IDEA HOW HARD IT IS TO HIDE *ONE* BILLION DOLLARS, MUCH LESS EIGHTY?
THE OTHER AUDITORS ONLY LOOK AT THE TOTALS. I LOOK AT *ALL* THE NUMBERS.

FINE. GIVE ME THE DECK.
THANK YOU.

LET ME GIVE YOU SOME UNSOLICITED ADVICE, IMALA.
DROP THIS.
THE DAY I HIRED YOU YOU SAID, "I'M APACHE. I'VE GOT SOME FIGHT IN ME." AND I RESPECT THAT.

BUT THIS ISN'T A FIGHT YOU WANT, IMALA. TAKING ON JUKE LIMITED IS LIKE TRYING TO TIE DOWN A GRIZZLY WITH DENTAL FLOSS. YOU'RE ONLY GOING TO PISS OFF THE BEAR.
TRUST THE GUYS ON YOUR TEAM. THEY'RE NOT AS STUPID AS YOU THINK.
BUT--
WE'RE AUDITORS, IMALA. IF YOU WANTED ADVENTURE, YOU SHOULD HAVE JOINED THE MILITARY.

PAPAKURA MILITARY CAMP, SOUTH AUCKLAND, NEW ZEALAND.
LIEUTENANT MAZER RACKHAM.
MEET CAPTAIN WIT O'TOOLE--AN AMERICAN. HE LEADS AN ELITE TEAM OF ALLIED SPECIAL FORCES CALLED THE MOBILE OPERATIONS POLICE OR MOPS.
I'D TELL YOU WHAT THEY DO EXACTLY, BUT THESE BOYS ARE WRAPPED IN SO MUCH HUSH HUSH, I HARDLY KNOW MYSELF.
YOUR COMMANDING OFFICER SAYS THAT YOU'RE THE BEST THIS NATION HAS TO OFFER.
I SERIOUSLY DOUBT THAT.
IF YOU WERE, HE WOULDN'T BE WILLING TO PART WITH YOU.
PART WITH ME, SIR?

MY TEAM HAS A VACANCY. YOUR C.O. THINKS YOU'RE THE MAN FOR THE JOB. I DISAGREE.
I'VE READ YOUR FILE. AND FROM THE LOOK OF YOU, I DON'T THINK YOU HAVE WHAT IT TAKES.
WITH ALL DUE RESPECT, SIR, A MAN'S LOOK AND FILE ARE RARELY AN ACCURATE MEASURE OF HIS CAPABILITIES.
THEN PROVE ME WRONG. TAKE OUR EVALUATION, THOUGH I SHOULD WARN YOU, IT'S NOT VERY PLEASANT.
I AM TRAINED FOR UNPLEASANT CONDITIONS, SIR.
WHEN DO WE BEGIN?
RIGHT NOW.
THE HELL?!

WAKE UP, MAZER.
SHOULD YOU EVER BE CAPTURED, THERE IS A HIGH PROBABILITY THAT YOU WOULD BE TORTURED.
THE DEVICE YOU'RE WEARING DIRECTLY STIMULATES VARIOUS BRAIN AREAS.
WITH IT, I CAN MAKE YOU EXPERIENCE AGONIZING PAIN, SEE BLINDING LIGHT, OR FEEL LIKE YOU NEED TO PEE SO BAD YOUR GUT WILL EXPLODE.

LET'S PRETEND YOU HAVE INFORMATION I WANT, SAY, THE NAME OF YOUR FIRST PET.
TELL ME THAT NAME NOW.

TORTURE? SERIOUSLY? THAT'S ALL YOU GOT?
VERY WELL.

AHH!!

SEVENTY-FOUR MINUTES LATER.
SEE THAT? I DIDN'T BREAK.
YES. VERY GOOD.
SO DID I PASS, O'TOOLE? AM I IN YOUR UNIT?
NO. NOBODY GETS IN MY UNIT UNLESS THEY BREAK OUT.
SUBMITTING TO TORTURE MEANS YOU ALREADY LOST ONCE. YOU HAVE TO HATE TO LOSE SO BADLY THAT YOU'D RATHER DIE TRYING TO ESCAPE. AND THEN BE GOOD ENOUGH TO ESCAPE WITHOUT DYING.
ANYONE IN MY UNIT WOULD HAVE OVERPOWERED THE GUARDS AND ESCAPED FROM THIS ROOM IN THREE MINUTES.
YOU JUST SAT THERE FOR AN HOUR.
SORRY, SOLDIER. YOU FAILED.
MARVELOUS.

WELL, THE HEATER'S FIXED.
FOR NOW, AT LEAST. I CAN'T DO A PERMANENT REPAIR UNTIL WE HAVE NEW PARTS.
WHICH WE CAN'T AFFORD UNTIL WE SELL SOME MINERALS.
I SEE TWO OPTIONS, VICTOR. ONE, WE TRY FOR A ROCK IN THE BELT AND PRAY ANOTHER CORPORATE DOESN'T BUMP US.
WE CAN'T SUSTAIN ANOTHER BUMP, CONCEPCION. PLAN B?
A REMOTE OBJECT. A ROCK FAR BEYOND THE BELT. WAY OUT IN OPEN SPACE WHERE NO ONE WILL BOTHER US.
HAS ANYONE EVER BEEN OUT THAT FAR?
LET'S HOPE NOT.

SIX WEEKS AND
300 MILLION MILES LATER.
<IT'LL BE A MIRACLE IF THOSE NETS HOLD.>
<VICTOR, COME LOOK AT THIS.>
<I'M GETTING SOMETHING ON THE HOLO. WAY OUT IN OPEN SPACE, MOVING NEAR THE SPEED OF LIGHT.>
<WHAT COULD BE MOVING THAT FAST? A COMET?>
<THAT'S JUST IT, VICTOR. *NOTHING* MOVES THAT FAST.>
<AND THAT'S NOT EVEN THE SCARY PART. WHAT REALLY FRIGHTENS ME IS THAT IT'S DECELERATING.>

"<AND HEADING STRAIGHT FOR US.>"

"No ship can move at the speed of light."

"I know that, Victor. I know what's possible and what isn't. I've been out here a lot longer than you have. If you have another explanation, I'm happy to hear it."

"Maybe it's not a ship, Concepción. Maybe it's a..."

"A what? Look at the readings. Look at the spectrograph. It has mass. It has a heat signature. This isn't a natural phenomenon. It's a vessel. With so much advanced tech the sensors can't even process most of the data output. And here, look at its trajectory."

"That's Earth."

"Yes, Victor. That is Earth."

From the recovered flight recorder of El Cavador, D-class mining vessel number 45F-781-6734G. Translated from Spanish.

PAPAKURA MILITARY CAMP, SOUTH AUCKLAND, NEW ZEALAND.
RANGE?
THREE THOUSAND FOUR HUNDRED AND SEVENTY-FIVE METERS.
BET SHE MISSES.
AT TWO MILES? PLEASE. PATU CAN HIT THAT IN HER SLEEP.
HOW WOULD YOU KNOW, FATANI? YOU WATCH HER SLEEP?
SHUT UP, REINHART.
BLAM
BOOM
NICE SHOT, PATU. YOU MUST HAVE REAL STEADY HANDS.
KEEP TALKING, REINHART, AND MY NEXT TARGET'S YOUR HEAD.
OOH. SASSY.
LIEUTENANT MAZER RACKHAM. COME IN, RACKHAM.

RACKHAM HERE.
LIEUTENANT, I WAS DISAPPOINTED TO HEAR THAT YOU FAILED THE MOPS EVALUATION.
I DESERVED TO FAIL, SIR. LESSON LEARNED.
FORGET IT. BLACK-OP TYPES ARE HEAD CASES ANYWAY. NEW ZEALAND SPECIAL AIR SERVICES NEEDS YOU HERE.
OR RATHER, IN CHINA.
CHINA, SIR?
NEW ORDERS. GET YOUR SQUAD TO THE AIRFIELD.
"YOU LEAVE IN TWO HOURS."

SOMEWHERE OVER THE SOUTH CHINA SEA.
THEY'RE CALLING IT A "DIPLOMATIC TRAINING EXERCISE." TWO ARMIES PLAYING NICE.
WE TEACH THE CHINESE TO FLY OUR NEW ATTACK HELICOPTERS. THEY TEACH US TO DRIVE A DIGGING VEHICLE THEY'VE DEVELOPED.
DIGGING VEHICLE?
WE GIVE THEM A CHOPPER. THEY GIVE US A *BULLDOZER?* LAME.
DOUBLE LAME.
I DON'T GET IT. ISN'T THIS SWAPPING SECRETS WITH THE ENEMY?
CHINA'S NOT OUR ENEMY, REINHART.
THEY'RE NOT OUR BEST FRIEND EITHER.
THEY ARE FOR THE NEXT SIX MONTHS. THAT'S OUR ORDERS.
THAT MEANS YOU, PATU--
--TRY NOT TO KILL ANYONE.

GUANGDONG PROVINCE, CHINA.
WELCOME TO CHINA, LIEUTENANT RACKHAM.
YOU COULD NOT HAVE TIMED YOUR ARRIVAL BETTER.
THE DRILL-SKIS WILL BE SURFACING MOMENTARILY.
SURFACING?

UM, THAT'S NOT A BULLDOZER.
I THINK I'M GOING TO LIKE CHINA AFTER ALL.
IT'S LIKE INVASION OF THE MOLE PEOPLE.

<IT COULD BE AN INVASION.>
EL CAVADOR MINING VESSEL. 300 MILLION MILES FROM EARTH.
<WE DON'T KNOW. ALL WE *DO* KNOW IS THAT THE SHIP WAS NOT MADE BY HUMANS.>
<WE HAVE TO WARN EVERYONE.>
<HOLD ON, CONCEPCIÓN. YOU'VE DETECTED A SHIP IN DEEP SPACE, MOVING AT *LIGHT SPEED?*>
<*NEAR* LIGHT SPEED, DAD. IT'S DECELERATING.>
<I KNOW IT SOUNDS CRAZY, UT THE SENSORS DON'T LIE. THIS THING IS ON A TRAJECTORY THROUGH THE ELT, STRAIGHT TO EARTH.>
<FINE. WE SEND A WARNING. OUR SIGNAL CAN REACH A RELAY STATION FROM HERE.>
<RIGHT?>

<WE'RE TOO FAR OUT.>
<AND EVEN IF WE COULD REACH A STATION, WE CAN'T BE SURE THE MESSAGE WOULD BE RELAYED. WHO WOULD BELIEVE IT?>
<VICTOR'S RIGHT. WE HAVE TO WARN EARTH IN PERSON. WITH EVIDENCE.>
<I SUGGEST WE SEND SOMEONE IN THE TUG.>
<IT'S NOT DESIGNED FOR ATMOSPHERIC REENTRY, BUT IT COULD LAND AT THE MOON. FROM THERE, A WARNING COULD BE SENT TO EARTH.>
<THE REST OF US WILL GO TO THE BELT AND WARN THEM THERE.>
<A ONE-MAN TUG TO THE MOON?>
<WHO'D BE CRAZY ENOUGH TO DO THAT?>
<ME.>

<TINY TUG.>
<NO MAGNETIC MANIPULATOR EITHER. SO NO GRAVITY. I'LL JUST FLOAT, EAT, AND SLEEP.>
<AND POOP AND PEE.>
<WELL, YEAH. GROSS.>
<WHAT'S THE METAL FOR?>
<SHIELD. FOR SOLAR RADIATION.>
<I DON'T WANT YOU TO GO, VICTOR.>
<WHAT IF THE ALIENS GET YOU?>
<HEY. NOBODY'S GOING TO GET ME, MONKEY BRAINS.>
<OR YOU. EVERYBODY'S GOING TO BE FINE. ALL RIGHT? I PROMISE.>

FOUR HOURS LATER.
<THE EVIDENCE IS ON THIS DATA CUBE.>
<GET IT TO THE RIGHT PEOPLE.>
<I WILL.>
<HERE.>
<FROM YOUR FATHER AND ME.>
<DON'T WATCH IT UNTIL YOU'RE A MILLION MILES OUT.>
<I'LL BE BACK IN A FEW MONTHS, MOTHER. YOU WON'T EVEN KNOW I'M GONE.>
<BE CAREFUL, SON.>
<AND REMEMBER...>
<"YOUR MOTHER AND I LOVE YOU.">

VICTOR. YOU'RE MY SON. THE LIGHT OF MY LIFE.
SO KNOW THAT IT IS WITH ALL THE LOVE I HAVE FOR YOU THAT I SAY THIS.
DON'T COME BACK.
UNDER THE SEAT YOU WILL FIND ENOUGH CREDITS TO ENROLL IN A UNIVERSITY ON EARTH.
IT'S NOT MUCH, BUT IT'S ALL WE HAVE.
CONCEPCIÓN ADDED HER SAVINGS AS WELL. YOUR MIND IS TOO VALUABLE TO WASTE IN THE BELT, SON.
MAKE US PROUD.

THE MOON.
OFFICES OF UKKO JUKES,
PRESIDENT AND CEO OF JUKE LIMITED.
MR. JUKES.
IMALA BOOTSTAMP FROM THE LUNAR TRADE DEPARTMENT HAS ARRIVED.
GOOD. SEND HER IN. AND GIVE HER A COM LINK.
YES, SIR.
EVER PLAYED GOLF, MS. BOOTSTAMP?
CAN'T SAY THAT I HAVE.
POWER AND PRECISION. THAT'S THE GAME.
COURSE, OUT HERE IN PARTIAL GRAVITY, WITH MAGNETIZED GOLF BALLS AND THIS RIDICULOUS SPACE SUIT--
I'M LUCKY TO HIT THE DAMN THING.

IT'S A GENTLEMEN'S GAME, YES.
BUT WOMEN COULD PLAY JUST AS WELL IF THEY PUT THEIR CONSIDERABLE MENTAL ENERGIES TO IT.
AND YOU, MS. BOOTSTAMP, STRIKE ME AS A WOMAN OF CONSIDERABLE MENTAL ENERGIES.
NATURALLY, I TREAT YOU EXACTLY AS I WOULD A MAN.
AND I TREAT YOU EXACTLY AS I WOULD A CRIMINAL.
IF YOU'VE BROUGHT ME HERE TO HUMILIATE AND INTIMIDATE ME, YOUR SPIES DON'T KNOW ME HALF AS WELL AS THEY THINK.
YOU MISJUDGE ME, MS. BOOTSTAMP.
I BROUGHT YOU HERE BECAUSE I AM CONCERNED ABOUT YOUR FUTURE.

MY STAFF INFORMS ME THAT YOU CONTINUE TO INVESTIGATE MY TRADE PRACTICES EVEN AFTER YOUR SUPERIOR ASKED YOU NOT TO DO SO.
THIS SEEMS AN UNWISE COURSE OF ACTION.
PARTICULARLY SINCE MY TRADE PRACTICES ARE IN FULL COMPLIANCE WITH YOUR DEPARTMENT'S STRICT REGULATIONS.
HARDLY.
I HAVE IRREFUTABLE EVIDENCE, MR. JUKES, THAT YOUR SHIPS HAVE BEEN EXCEEDING WEIGHT LIMITS FOR TRANSSHIPMENTS TO EARTH--
--YEAR AFTER YEAR, WITHOUT PAYING THE REQUIRED FEES AND FINES.
IRREFUTABLE, YOU SAY?
WELL NOW, THAT IS TROUBLING. I'LL LOOK INTO THIS MATTER PERSONALLY.
THANK YOU FOR BRINGING IT TO MY ATTENTION.

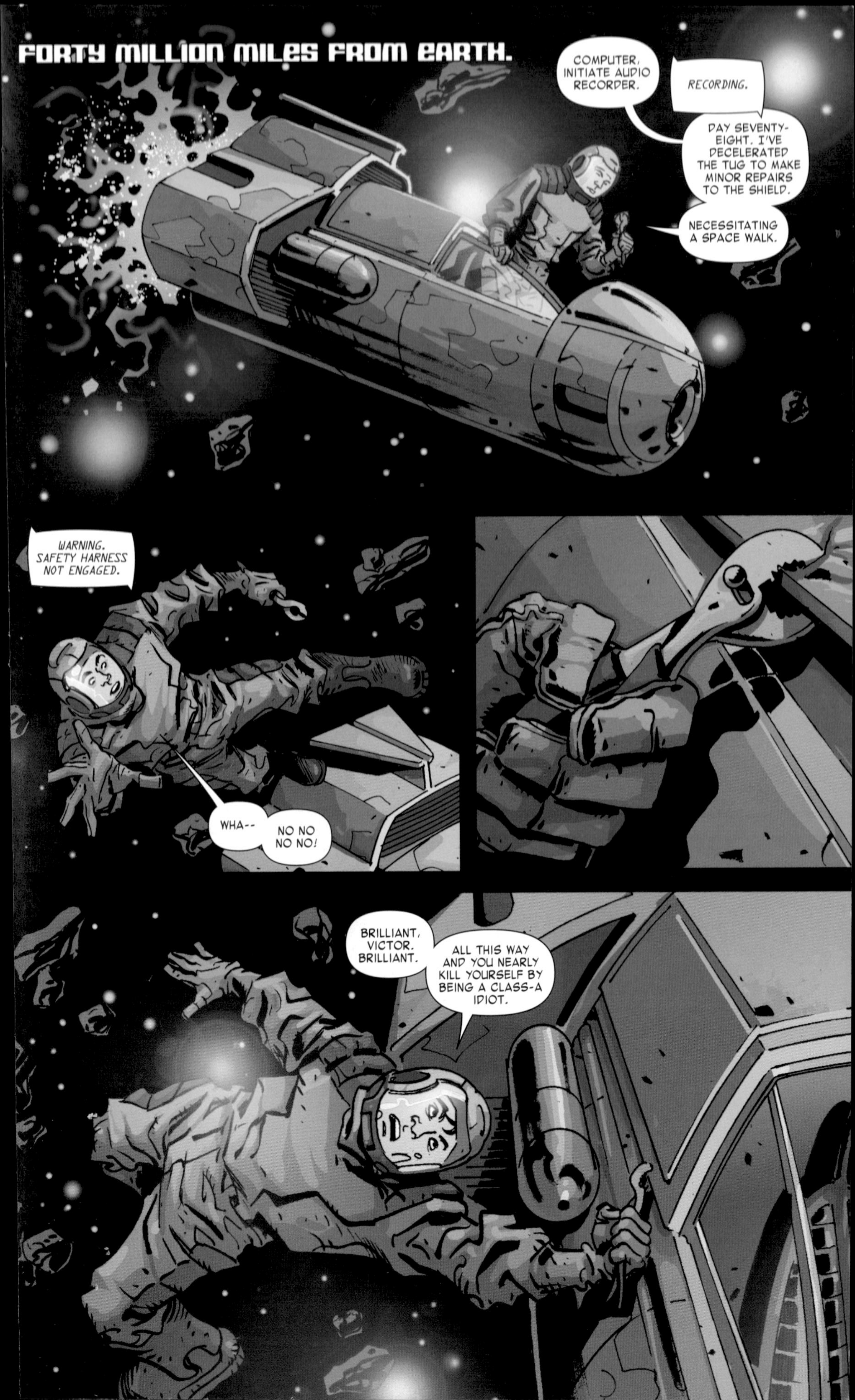
FORTY MILLION MILES FROM EARTH.
COMPUTER, INITIATE AUDIO RECORDER.
RECORDING.
DAY SEVENTY-EIGHT. I'VE DECELERATED THE TUG TO MAKE MINOR REPAIRS TO THE SHIELD.
NECESSITATING A SPACE WALK.
WARNING. SAFETY HARNESS NOT ENGAGED.
WHA--
NO NO NO NO!
BRILLIANT, VICTOR. BRILLIANT.
ALL THIS WAY AND YOU NEARLY KILL YOURSELF BY BEING A CLASS-A IDIOT.

INITIATE DIAGNOSTIC.
CLOSE ENOUGH.
SHIELD STRENGTH AT NINETY-NINE POINT NINE SEVEN PERCENT.
HOW MUCH LONGER BEFORE THE ALIEN VESSEL REACHES THE BELT, ASSUMING DECELERATION AND CURRENT FLIGHT PATH REMAIN CONSTANT?
INSUFFICIENT DATA. SPECIFY BELT LOCATION.
WEIGH STATION FOUR.
THIRTY-SEVEN DAYS. FOUR HOURS.
THEN WE NEED TO HAUL.
MAXIMUM ACCELERATION ENGAGED.

WEIGH STATION FOUR, THE BELT.
THIRTY-SIX DAYS LATER.
Olo Video
BAR
GIRLS IN ZERO.G
A TOAST.
TO THE VENEZUELAN FREE MINERS WHO SO GRACIOUSLY GAVE US THEIR DIG SITE.
JUKE
AND TO OUR WISE CAPTAIN, LEM JUKES--
--FOR HAULING IN THREE HUNDRED THOUSAND TONS OF IRON WITHOUT SPILLING A SINGLE ROCK.
HEAR HEAR.
THAT'LL SHOW YOUR OLD MAN, LEM.

OH YOU'RE WRONG THERE, CHUBS.
NOTHING'S GOOD ENOUGH FOR OLD IRON BALLS, UKKO JUKES.
WHY LEM HERE COULD LASSO JUPITER, AND HIS OLD MAN WOULD HUFF AND SCOWL AND SAY--
"THAT'S IT? ONLY ONE PLANET?"
"YOU DISAPPOINT ME, SON. DIS-A-POINT!"
HEY, I LOVE MY DAD.
WHO ELSE WOULD WE STEAL CREDITS FROM?
HA HA HA HA HA HA HA HA HA HA

LUNAR TRADE DEPARTMENT.
YOU DON'T UNDERSTAND, IMALA. I HAVE NO CHOICE BUT TO DEMOTE YOU?
WE HAVE A SYSTEM HERE, IMALA. AN ORDER FOR DOING THINGS.
YOU GOING ROGUE LIKE THIS IS UNSETTLING A LOT OF PEOPLE.
PEOPLE LIKE UKKO JUKES?
DON'T ARGUE. YOU'RE LUCKY TO HAVE THIS NEW JOB. THE BOYS UPSTAIRS WANTED TO FIRE YOU OUTRIGHT.
YOU'RE GOING TO LET UKKO JUKES BULLY YOU?
BECAUSE JUKES HAS THEM IN HIS POCKET!

I STUCK MY NECK OUT FOR YOU, IMALA. NOW TAKE THE JOB AND AT LEAST ACT GRATEFUL.
DON'T THINK OF IT AS GIVING UP.
THINK OF IT AS NOT GETTING SHIPPED BACK TO EARTH UNEMPLOYED.
ALL RIGHT.
WHAT IS IT?
CUSTOMS. WORKING WITH PEOPLE, WHICH I KNOW YOU HATE.
YOUR FIRST CASE IS A GUY WHO SHOWED UP A FEW HOURS AGO ON MOON DOCK 10.
CAME IN ON A TUG. NO DOCUMENTATION. NO AUTHORIZED FLIGHT PATH.
DEAL WITH IT.

WHY DON'T YOU HAVE ANY IDENTIFICATION, MISTER...?
DELGADO. VICTOR DELGADO.
LOOK, YOU'RE WASTING MY TIME. ISN'T THERE SOMEONE ABOVE YOU I CAN SPEAK WITH?
OF COURSE.
BUT YOU DON'T SEE THAT PERSON UNLESS I SAY SO. AND I *DON'T* SAY SO.
NOW PLEASE ANSWER THE QUESTION.
I DON'T HAVE I.D. BECAUSE I WAS **BORN** IN THE BELT. I'M A FREE MINER.
AND I HAVE INFORMATION THAT NEEDS--
--TO BE SENT TO EARTH. YES, YES.
SOMETHING ABOUT A--HOW DID YOU PHRASE IT?--"ALIEN VESSEL."
LET ME GUESS, THERE'S NO PROOF OF THAT EITHER.
ACTUALLY, THAT I *DO* HAVE.

ONE HOUR LATER.
THIS HAS TO BE A HOAX.
YES, THAT'S IT. A BIG, ELABORATE HOAX.
I WENT OUT AND INVENTED A *LIGHT-SPEED SHIP* JUST SO I COULD PRANK YOU.
LADY, IF YOU DON'T GET OFF YOUR DUFF AND LET ME TALK WITH SOMEONE *IMPORTANT*--
--YOU'RE GOING TO BECOME ONE OF THOSE NEWS STORIES ABOUT HOW WE *DID* GET EARLY WARNING BUT SOME LOW-LEVEL, TIME-SERVING BUREAUCRAT BURIED IT!
BUT I SUGGEST YOU ACT QUICKLY.
THE *"ALIEN VESSEL"* COULD BE AT THE BELT...

"...RIGHT NOW."

TAN
GURU-eFX

"We don't even know what the hull is composed of, Concepción. Carbon steel? Titanium? An impenetrable metal alloy we've never even heard of? And how thick is it? Quarter of an inch? Ninety feet? A mile? Who's to say a few mining explosives will do anything but scratch the paint job?"

"You saw what it did to Weigh Station Four, Lem."

"Which is why your idea sounds like suicide."

"But it wasn't attacking Weigh Station Four. It was brushing it aside. Weigh Station Four was destroyed because it was in the way. It sat along the ship's trajectory. Or at least close to it. It was an obstacle, nothing more."

"If this is supposed to reassure me, you're failing miserably."

"Collision-avoidance systems, Lem. The ship must have automatic systems to protect its hull from impact with objects in space."

"What's your point?"

"My point is, that ship can bleed. If the hull was impenetrable, if it was impervious to a sudden, violent impact, why would it need a collision avoidance system?"

From the recovered flight recorder of El Cavador, D-Class mining vessel number 45F-781-6734G. Translated From Spanish.

WEIGH STATION FOUR. THE KUIPER BELT.
<WE'RE TOO LATE.>
<THE ALIEN SHIP HAS ALREADY COME THROUGH HERE.>
<IT...IT DESTROYED EVERYTHING. THE WHOLE STATION. ALL THOSE PEOPLE-->
< ESTEBEN, WHERE'S THE SHIP NOW?>
<AHEAD OF US, STILL ON ITS TRAJECTORY TO EARTH.>
<AND IT HAS SLOWED DOWN DRASTICALLY. AND I MEAN WAY DOWN. IT'S NOW HOLDING AT SIXTY THOUSAND MILES PER HOUR.>
EL CAVADOR, D-CLASS MINING VESSEL.
<CAN WE CATCH IT?>
<MAYBE. WE'RE AT SEVENTY THOUSAND MILES PER HOUR.>
<TAKE US UP TO SEVENTY-FIVE AND SET US ON A COURSE TO INTERCEPT THE ALIEN SHIP.>
<WE'RE NOT STOPPING?>
<THERE COULD BE PEOPLE DOWN THERE WHO NEED HELP.>
<TWELVE BILLION PEOPLE ON EARTH ARE GOING TO NEED HELP IF WE DON'T STOP THAT SHIP.>

<HOW MANY MINING SHIPS IN THE VICINITY ARE MOVING IN THE SAME DIRECTION AND SIMILAR SPEED AS WE ARE?>
<I'VE GOT TEN SHIPS IN FRONT OF US.>
<BUT ONLY TWO ARE MATCHING OUR SPEED.>
<WE CAN'T WAIT FOR THE OTHERS TO ACCELERATE. WE'D NEVER CATCH THE ALIEN SHIP.>
<WHAT ARE THE TWO SHIPS?>
<ONE'S A WU-HU. DRILL SHIP.>
<THE OTHER IS LEM JUKE'S SHIP.>
<HAIL THEM. USE THE LASER COM, NOT THE RADIO.>
<LEM JUKES? HE CRIPPLED OUR SHIP. HE KILLED MARCOS. HE'S A MURDERER. WE DON'T WANT HIS HELP.>
<WE NEED ALL THE HELP WE CAN GET.>

CHINESE MINING VESSEL, B-CLASS.
PROPERTY: WU-HU INTERNATIONAL.
WE CAN INTERCEPT WITH YOU, CAVADOR.
龍 1Z
BUT I AM UNDER STRICT ORDERS NOT TO ASSIST OR COLLABORATE WITH A JUKES VESSEL.
THEY'RE OUR PRIMARY COMPETITOR.
YOU'VE SEEN OUR IMAGES OF WEIGH STATION FOUR, CAPTAIN.
WHAT'S LEFT OF IT, YES.
THEN YOU'LL AGREE THAT THIS IS HARDLY THE TIME FOR CORPORATE POLITICS.
NAVIGATOR, CHANGE COURSE TO EL CAVADOR'S RENDEZVOUS COORDINATES.
YES, SIR.

CORPORATE MINING VESSEL, A-CLASS. PROPERTY: JUKES LTD.
CARGO BAY.
DID YOU REALLY THINK THAT KNOCKING ASIDE A DINKY SHIP OF FREE MINERS WOULD IMPRESS ME, LEM?
YOU ARE CARRYING OUR ONLY PROTOTYPE GRAVITY LASER. THAT DRILL IS WORTH MORE THAN TWENTY SHIPS!
YOU COULD HAVE DAMAGED IT!
AND FOR WHAT? A MERE THREE HUNDRED THOUSAND TONS OF ROCK?
I WISH THIS WASN'T A TIME-DELAYED MESSAGE. I WISH I COULD TELL YOU TO YOUR FACE HOW ENORMOUSLY STUPID AND ASININE--
END TRANSMISSION.

DEAR OLD DAD. WHAT A CHARMER.
YOU HAVE ANOTHER TRANSMISSION IN YOUR QUEUE. SHALL I PLAY IT?
IF IT'S FROM MY FATHER, DELETE IT.
NEGATIVE. TRANSMISSION ORIGINATES FROM A MINING VESSEL, CALL SIGN EL CAVADOR.
PLAY IT.
LEM JUKES, I HOPED OUR PATHS WOULD NEVER CROSS AGAIN, BUT CIRCUMSTANCES DEMAND IT.
WEIGH STATION FOUR HAS BEEN DESTROYED.
I AM SENDING YOU ALL THE DATA YOU NEED.
FORWARD THAT TRANSMISSION AND DATA TO THE BRIDGE IMMEDIATELY.

AN ALIEN SHIP?
THIS CAN'T BE REAL.
THIS IS BOGUS, RIGHT?
OPEN A FREQUENCY TO EL CAVADOR.
JUKE
I GOT YOUR MESSAGE. WHAT DO YOU SUGGEST?
I'VE GIVEN YOU COORDINATES TO A RENDEZVOUS, THREE DAYS FROM YOUR CURRENT POSITION.
WE'LL DOCK, MEET HERE ON EL CAVADOR, AND DISCUSS WHAT ACTION WE SHOULD TAKE.
MEET ON YOUR SHIP?
HOW DO I KNOW THIS ISN'T A TRICK?
YOU COULD BE PLANNING TO GUT ME WITH A PICK AXE, FOR ALL I KNOW.
BELIEVE ME, MR. JUKES.
IF I WANTED REVENGE, YOU WOULD ALREADY BE DEAD.

THREE DAYS LATER.
WE'LL COME ALONGSIDE THE SHIP AND SET CHARGES ON ITS HULL.
AT SIXTY THOUSAND MILES PER HOUR?
IT'S NOT GOING TO STOP FOR US, IF THAT'S WHAT YOU'RE ASKING.
MY MEN AREN'T TRAINED FOR EXPLOSIVES. WE'RE DRILL OPERATORS.
MY MEN WILL SET THE CHARGES.
HALF OF THEM WILL COME WITH EL CAVADOR TO THE STARBOARD SIDE. LEM WILL TAKE THE OTHER HALF AND ATTACK PORT.
THE WU-HU SHIP WILL MONITOR FROM A SAFE DISTANCE WITH ALL OF THE WOMEN AND CHILDREN FROM EL CAVADOR.

WHY DON'T *I* GET THE WOMEN AND CHILDREN? THE WU-HU SHIP'S BETTER EQUIPPED FOR AN ATTACK THAN *WE* ARE.
NONE OF US ARE EQUIPPED TO ATTACK, LEM. WE'RE *MINING* VESSELS.
YOU HAVE A HARPOON AND WINCH. THE WU-HU DOESN'T.
WE NEED YOU TO SECURE ONE OF THE CABLES.
WE'LL RELY ON THE COMM LINKS IN THE SUITS TO COMMUNICATE. NOT RADIO.
WHY NOT?
BECAUSE THEY MIGHT BE ABLE TO DETECT IT. THEY'D KNOW WE WERE THERE.
WHAT IF THEY HAVE SENSORS ON THEIR HULL? WHAT IF THEY CAN DETECT MOVEMENT?
THEN IT'S GOING TO BE A VERY SHORT FIGHT.

ONE AT A TIME, PLEASE, IN AN ORDERLY FASHION.
AREN'T YOU COMING WITH US ON THE WU-HU SHIP?
I SAID "WOMEN AND CHILDREN," MONO, NOT "OLD WOMEN AND CHILDREN." I'LL BE FINE HERE.
YOU DO YOUR BUSINESS AND COME BACK TO ME, SEGUNDO. YOU HEAR ME?
I'VE BEEN HOGGING THE COVERS AND ANNOYING YOU FOR THIRTY YEARS, RENA.
YOU THINK I'M GOING TO STOP NOW, JUST WHEN I GOT THE HANG OF IT?
SETTING CHARGES IS CAKE WORK.
I'LL BE BACK BEFORE YOU KNOW IT.
THAT'S EVERYONE. LET'S SEAL THE HATCH.

LEM'S SHIP IS IN POSITION. THIS IS IT.
REMEMBER, YOUR SUITS WEREN'T DESIGNED FOR SPACE WALKS AT THIS SPEED.
THEY'LL PROTECT YOU FROM COLLISIONS WITH SPACE DUST--
--BUT ANYTHING BIGGER WILL RIP THROUGH YOU LIKE SHRAPNEL.
SO THE LESS TIME YOU SPEND OUTSIDE, THE BETTER.
BOTTOM LINE? MOVE FAST.
SET THE CHARGES. CLICK BACK ON THE CABLE, AND I'LL REEL YOU IN.
NOTHING TO IT.
RIGHT. NOTHING TO IT. PERFORM A SPACE WALK AT AN INSANE SPEED, TAKE OUT A MURDEROUS ALIEN SHIP, AND NOT DIE.
EASY.

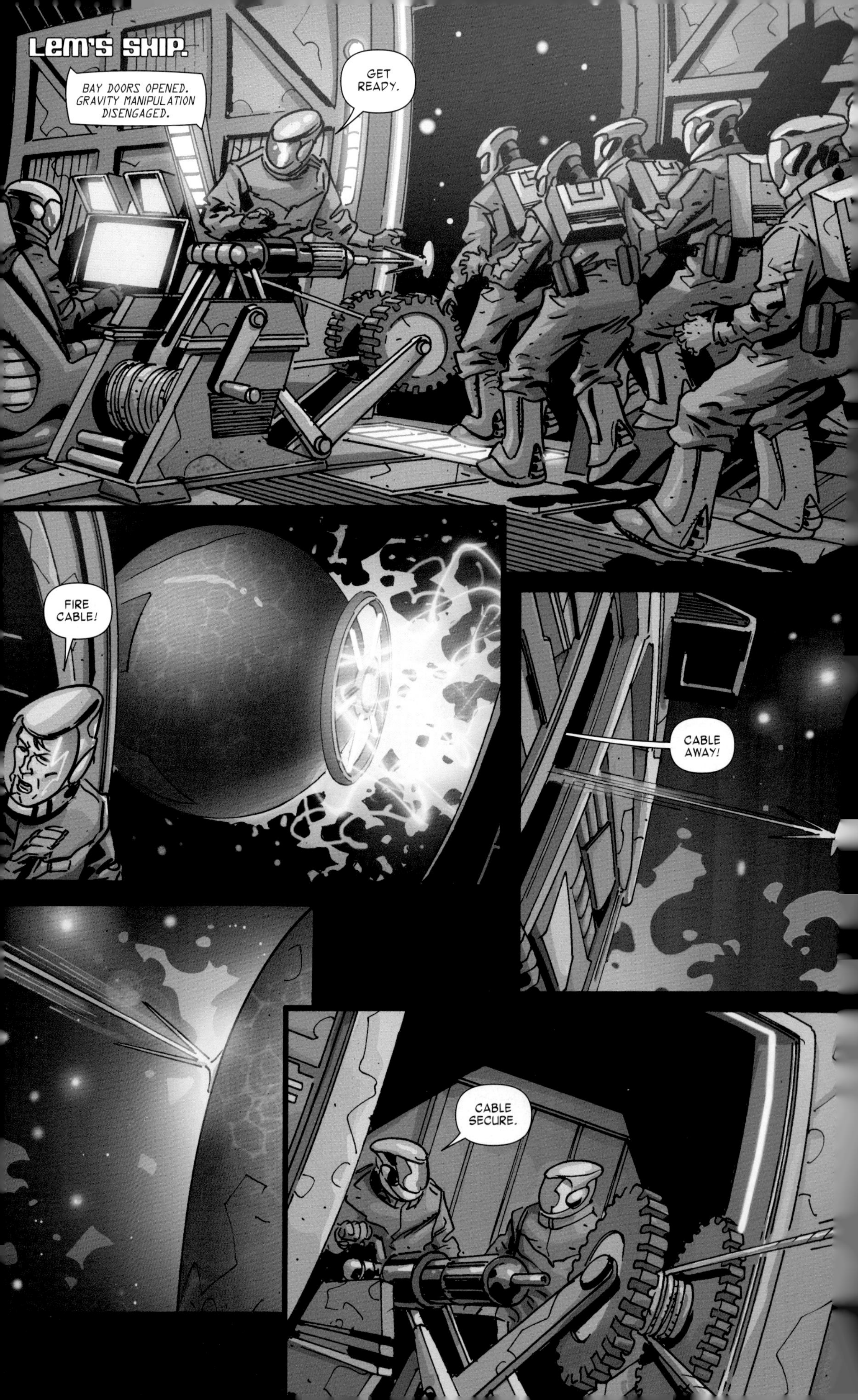
LEM'S SHIP.
BAY DOORS OPENED. GRAVITY MANIPULATION DISENGAGED.
GET READY.
FIRE CABLE!
CABLE AWAY!
CABLE SECURE.

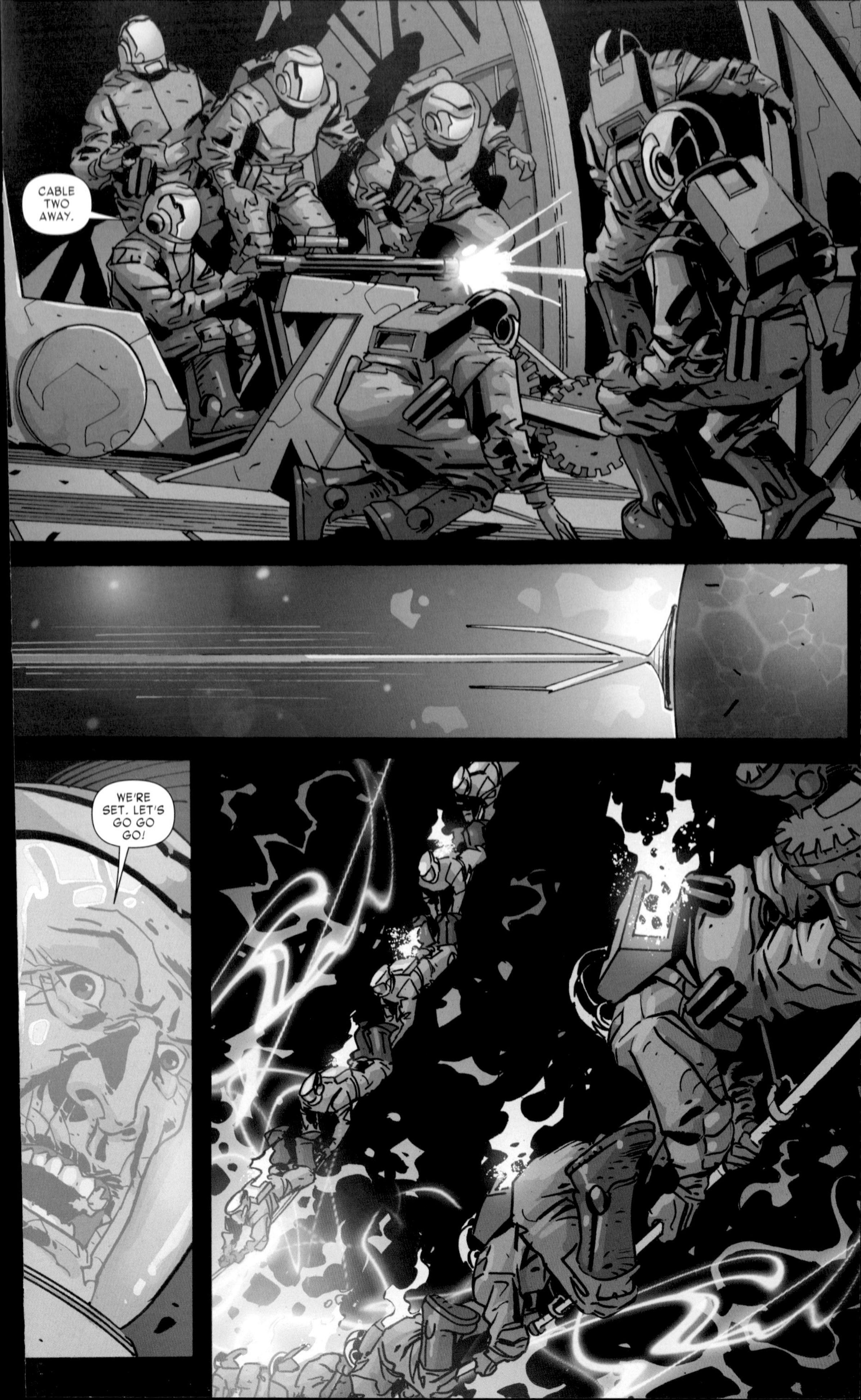
CABLE TWO AWAY.
WE'RE SET. LET'S GO GO GO!

THESE HAND MAGNETS HAD BETTER WORK, SEGUNDO, OR WE GOT NOTHING TO HOLD ON TO.

ALL RIGHT. SPREAD OUT, WE WANT TO MAXIMIZE THE DAMAGE.

FORTY-FIVE MINUTE TIMERS. WE WANT TO GIVE OURSELVES PLENTY OF TIME TO GET OUT OF HERE.
45:00

SEGUNDO. I GOT A GLITCH IN MY TIMER. CAN'T SET THE MECHANISM. I'M WORRIED IT MIGHT GO OFF BEFORE WE CAN--

SEGUNDO! WHAT HAPPENED?
CHARGE WENT OFF PREMATURELY.
IT WAS ESTEBAN.
HE'S DEAD.
SET THE REMAINING CHARGES NOW AND GET BACK TO THE CABLES. FORGET ABOUT SPREADING OUT.
THERE'S SOMETHING MOVING DOWN IN THAT HOLE.
SEGUNDO, GET THE MEN BACK TO THE CABLES, NOW!
EVERYBODY, GET BACK!
WHAT THE HELL IS THAT?

NO!

THEY'RE RIPPING OFF THE CHARGES!

AAAHHH!
THEY'RE PEELING OUR MEN OFF THE SHIP. THEY'RE SACRIFICING THEMSELVES.

REEL US IN!
CUT THE CABLE.
WHAT! NO, THEY'LL DIE!
I'M REELING THEM IN.

CUT THE CABLE NOW!
WE'VE ALMOST GOT THEM.

CUT. THE. CABLE.
CARGO BAY SEALED.
GET US OUT OF HERE!
WE CAN'T LEAVE EL CAVADOR!
WATCH ME.

WHOA.
SNAP ON! I'M PULLING YOU UP!

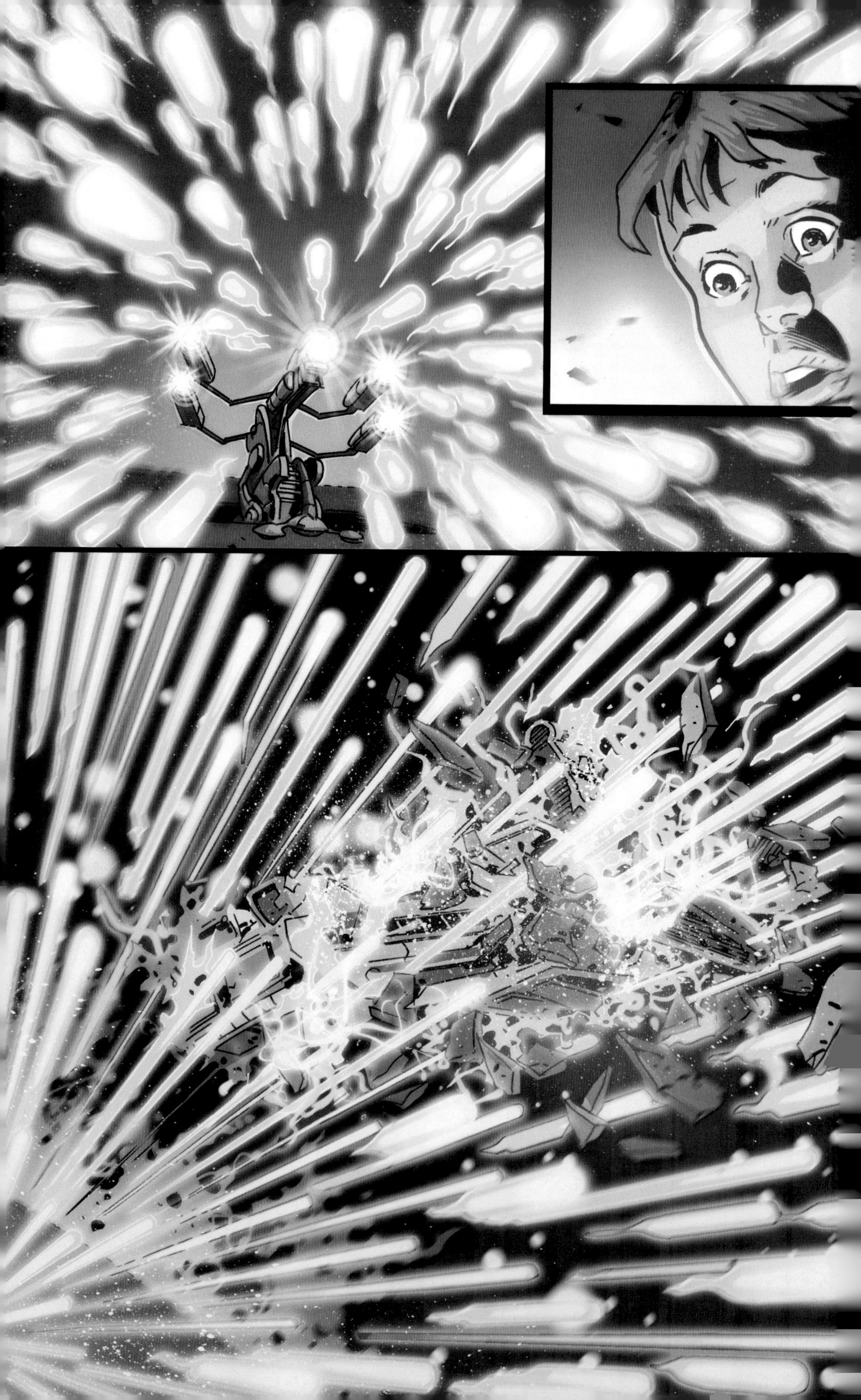

FSSSS
RENA, I DON'T KNOW IF YOU CAN HEAR ME, BUT MY SUIT IS PUNCTURED AND LEAKING OXYGEN.
FSSSS

EVEN IF THE WU-HU SHIP DECELERATED NOW AND YOU KNEW EXACTLY WHERE TO FIND ME, YOU'D STILL NOT REACH ME IN TIME.

SO DON'T STOP.
GO SOMEWHERE SAFE.
THAT'S ALL I ASK. SURVIVE.

AND NEVER FORGET THAT I LOVE YOU.

GURU-eFX

"Hey Wolheim, I'm getting some weird noise over the HF bands across all spectrums."

"Interference?"

"Big time. I can't radio anybody. And I got boys at the dig site awaiting orders."

"You check the switched-mode power supply?"

"I checked everything."

"Try a simple diode detector with an s-meter instead of the speaker."

"You think I'm sleeping over here? I told you. I tried everything."

"Must be something outside. A passing ship, maybe?"

"No way. No ship could carry that much power."

"Bring up a visual of space, say within four hundred kilometers of us."

"OK, but I'm telling you, nothing could . . ."

"What the devil is that?"

—Final transcript from Delta Radio Tower, Juke Limited Mining Complex South, Asteroid 216 Kleopatra.

"RENA... SUIT IS PUNCTURED."
WU-XU MINING VESSEL. KUIPER BELT.
"...NOT REACH ME IN TIME... NEVER FORGET..."
I'M SORRY, MRS. DELGADO. BUT WE ONLY RECEIVED BITS AND PIECES OF YOUR HUSBAND'S TRANSMISSION BEFORE WE LOST ALL COMMUNICATIONS.
CONSIDERING HOW MUCH TIME HAS PASSED SINCE THE INCIDENT, I'M AFRAID WE MUST ASSUME THE WORST.
YOU HAVE MY MOST SINCERE CONDOLENCES.
LIEUTENANT. SEE TO IT THAT MRS. DELGADO IS GIVEN EVERY COMFORT. THEN FIND SOMEONE AMONG THE CREW WITH GRIEF-COUNSELING TRAINING.
I WANT EVERY WOMAN AND CHILD FROM EL CAVADOR GIVEN DUE ATTENTION AND RESPECT.
YES, SIR.

SO WE CAN'T TRANSMIT AT ALL?
NO, SIR. WE DON'T HAVE SHIELDING ON OUR COMMUNICATIONS, AND THE ALIEN SHIP WAS EMITTING ALL KINDS OF INTERFERENCE.
WE WERE LUCKY TO PICK UP THAT TRANSMISSION FROM THE MINER.
THE MOMENT WE'RE BACK ONLINE, I WANT TO SEND ALL THE VIDEO WE TOOK OF THE SKIRMISH WITH THE ALIENS DIRECTLY TO CORPORATE HEADQUARTERS.
AS LONG AS IT GETS THERE BEFORE THAT SHIP DOES.
THAT WILL TAKE TIME TO REACH EARTH, SIR. WE'RE VERY FAR OUT.
ARE WE SURE THIS THING IS DEAD?
IT WAS DEAD BEFORE WE FOUND IT, SIR. THEY'RE NO MORE IMMUNE TO THE VACUUM OF SPACE THAN WE ARE.
I DON'T WANT THIS THING JERKING AWAKE ON MY SHIP, DOCTOR.
RELAX, CAPTAIN. NOTHING CAN SURVIVE A THOROUGH AUTOPSY.

WHAT IS IT?
THEY'RE SEMI-VERTEBRATE, IN THAT THEY HAVE A SINGLE NEURAL COLUMN, BUT CLEARLY THEY EVOLVED FROM EXO-SKELETAL HEXIFORMS.
WHAT DOES THAT MEAN?
THEY EVOLVED FROM CREATURES VERY MUCH LIKE ANTS, BUT THEY LEFT ANTHOOD FAR BEHIND.
BUT THEY CAN BE KILLED?
NOT EASILY, PERHAPS. THEY'RE QUITE STRONG.
BUT YES, THEY MOST DEFINITELY CAN BE KILLED.

ELSEWHERE.
JUKE LTD 45-BY
I'M TRYING, LEM, BUT OUR RADIO'S IN THE TOILET.
THAT SHIP'S PUTTING OFF MAJOR INTERFERENCE.
WHAT ABOUT THE CORPORATE LASER-LINE? CAN WE SEND A MESSAGE THAT WAY?
AT THIS SPEED? THAT'S LIKE SHOOTING DOWN A HOUSEFLY FROM A GALLOPING HORSE. IT'D BE A MIRACLE IF WE HIT A RECEIVER.
THEN GIVE ME A MIRACLE.
LEM, MAYBE WE SHOULD SLOW DOWN, YOU KNOW. WHAT GOOD IS IT CHASING THIS THING?
THAT "THING" HAS KILLED HUNDREDS OF PEOPLE.
HEY LEM, YOU BETTER LOOK AT THIS.

IT'S SPEEDING UP?
YEAH. BOOKIN'. BUT THAT'S NOT THE WORST OF IT.
AND?
I CHECKED ITS FLIGHT PATH WITH THIS NEW SPEED TO SEE IF IT WOULD PASS NEAR ANYTHING BEFORE IT REACHES EARTH.
IT DOES.
ASTEROID 216 KLEOPATRA.
THAT'S ONE OF MY FATHER'S ROCKS.
JUKE
MORE THAN A ROCK, LEM. IT'S AN ENTIRE MINING COMPLEX, WITH BARRACKS AND EVERYTHING.
HOW MANY PEOPLE?
OVER FIVE HUNDRED.
WE NEED TO GET A MESSAGE TO MY FATHER.
LIKE NOW.

THE MOON.
I THOUGHT WE WERE TRYING TO WARN EARTH, IMALA.
WE ARE, VICTOR. BUT WE CAN'T JUST WALK INTO THE U.N. OR S.T.A.S.A. AND EXPECT THEM TO LISTEN TO US. WE NEED MORE EVIDENCE.
S.T.A.S.A.?
SPACE TRADE AND SECURITY AUTHORITY. THEY'VE GOT THE EAR OF EVERY POLITICIAN AND NEWS ORGANIZATION IN THE WORLD.
THEN WHY ARE WE GOING TO UKKO JUKES? HE'S A CORPORATE JERK. HE'S NOT S.T.A.S.A.
LOOK, I DON'T LIKE UKKO ANY MORE THAN YOU DO, PROBABLY EVEN LESS.
BUT ON THE MOON, UKKO HAS THE TELESCOPES. IF WE CAN GET PHOTOS OF THIS SHIP, PEOPLE WILL TAKE US SERIOUSLY.
YOU STILL DON'T BELIEVE ME, DO YOU?
DO YOU THINK I'D PUT MY CRIPPLED CAREER AT RISK, VICTOR, IF I DIDN'T BELIEVE YOU?

JUKE LTD
MINING THE FUTURE
WHAT'S WRONG WITH THE EVIDENCE WE ALREADY HAVE?
DO YOU KNOW HOW MANY WHACKOS GO TO S.T.A.S.A. EVERY YEAR WITH FUZZY HOME VIDEOS, CLAIMING TO HAVE DISCOVERED AN ALIEN SPACECRAFT?
BUT WE *HAVE* DISCOVERED AN ALIEN SPACECRAFT.
SAYS YOU. TO THEM, WE'RE CRAZY NOBODIES, ONE OF WHOM ISN'T EVEN AN *OFFICIAL* NOBODY BECAUSE HE DOESN'T HAVE IDENTIFICATION *OR* CITIZENSHIP.
WHAT MAKES YOU THINK UKKO WILL EVEN GIVE US THE TIME OF DAY?
HE HATES ME. IF I GO BEGGING TO HIM, HE'LL GIVE US AN AUDIENCE JUST TO AMUSE HIMSELF.
WAIT.
HE *HATES* YOU?

SOMEWHERE IN INDIA.
TALK TO US, COMPUTER.
YOUR TARGET, CAPTAIN WIT O'TOOLE, IS THREE THOUSAND SEVEN HUNDRED AND FOUR METERS NORTH OF YOUR POSITION.
NIGHT NIGHT, PRETTY BRITCHES.
POP

DISTANCE TO TARGET: FORTY-THREE METERS.
TWENTY METERS.
SEVEN METERS.

BANG.
YOU'RE DEAD.

WELL DONE, GENTLEMEN.
NOW GATHER THE OTHERS. IT'S TIME TO CHANGE THE RULES OF THE GAME.

MOPS TRAINING FACILITY.
WHAT DID WE LEARN FROM THIS EXERCISE?
THAT NOTHING CAN STOP THE MOPS!
PLEASE. WE LET YOU TURKEYS WIN.
YOU HEAR THAT, BOYS. B TEAM IS A LITTLE MIFFED THEY GOT THEIR BUTTS HANDED TO THEM.
SUCK IT UP, LOSERS.
YOU WON'T EVEN GET CLOSE TO THE CAPTAIN WHEN IT'S OUR TURN TO BE THE SENTRIES.
WHAT WE LEARNED, GENTLEMEN, IS THAT WE'VE BECOME TOO RELIANT UPON OUR EQUIPMENT.
FROM NOW ON, FUTURE EXERCISES WILL BE CONDUCTED WITH NO TECH WEAPONS OR GUIDANCE SYSTEMS.
NO TECH? AGAINST AN ARMED ENEMY?
WHO'S TO SAY WE WILL ALWAYS HAVE THE TECHNOLOGICAL ADVANTAGE?
WE'RE NOT SOLDIERS UNTIL WE KNOW HOW TO GO STARK NAKED AGAINST A FULLY ARMED ENEMY AND KILL HIM.

THE MOON.
MR. JUKES, THIS SHIP IS COMING WHETHER WE WARN THE WORLD OR NOT.
AND IF IT PROVES HOSTILE, AND YOU, A MAN OF RESOURCES, IGNORE IT, HISTORY WILL BE NONE TOO KIND. YOU'D BE BRANDED A COWARD OR TRAITOR TO THE HUMAN RACE.
SPARE ME THE MELODRAMA, MS. BOOTSTAMP. I ALREADY KNOW THE SHIP IS HOSTILE.
WHAT?
YOU KNEW ABOUT IT?
AND YOU DID NOTHING?
WE LEARNED OF IT ONLY THIS MORNING. I RECEIVED A LASER-LINE FROM MY SON. HE WAS INVOLVED IN A SKIRMISH WITH THIS SHIP.
WHAT ABOUT MY FAMILY? EL CAVADOR? DID HE SAY ANYTHING ABOUT MY FAMILY?
PLEASE. WE DON'T KEEP TRACK OF SCAVENGERS.

MR. JUKES.
I TOLD YOU I WAS NOT TO BE DISTURBED.
I GUARANTEE YOU, SIR, YOU'LL WANT TO SEE THIS.
A CLOUD OF SPACE DUST? HOW FASCINATING.
NO, SIR.
THIS IS WHAT IS LEFT OF YOUR ASTEROID KLEOPATRA AND THE FIVE HUNDRED AND EIGHTY-THREE EMPLOYEES WHO WORKED THERE.

LADIES AND GENTLEMEN OF THE PRESS.
PEOPLE OF EARTH--
WE ARE NOT ALONE IN THE UNIVERSE.
WHITE HOUSE.
AN INTELLIGENT AND HOSTILE ALIEN SPECIES IS AT THIS VERY MOMENT APPROACHING EARTH IN A SHIP UNLIKE ANYTHING WE'VE EVER SEEN.
MR. PRESIDENT, THE DIRECTOR OF S.T.A.S.A. IS ON LINE ONE.

THESE IMAGES AND VIDEO FOOTAGE, WHICH I HAVE SUPPLIED TO S.T.A.S.A., LEAVE NO DOUBT IN MY MIND THAT OUR PLANET IS IN GRAVE DANGER.

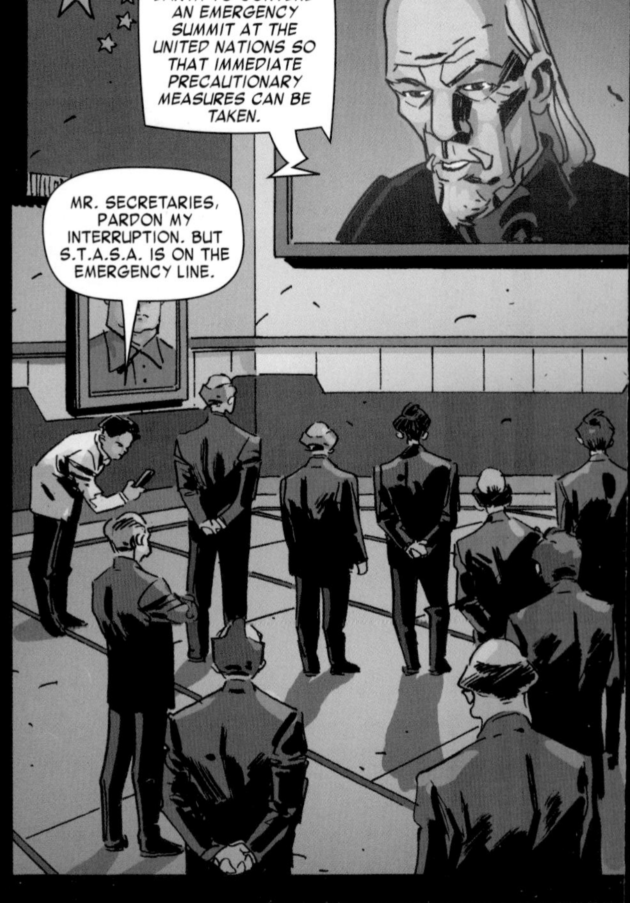
OFFICE OF THE POLITBURO, BEIJING.
I CALL UPON ALL GOVERNMENTS OF EARTH TO CONVENE AN EMERGENCY SUMMIT AT THE UNITED NATIONS SO THAT IMMEDIATE PRECAUTIONARY MEASURES CAN BE TAKEN.
MR. SECRETARIES, PARDON MY INTERRUPTION. BUT S.T.A.S.A. IS ON THE EMERGENCY LINE.

TWENTY-FOUR HOURS LATER.
KENWE ZUBEKA, DIRECTOR OF ALIEN AFFAIRS FOR THE UNITED NATIONS, A POST WITH FEW DEMANDS PRIOR TO YESTERDAY'S SHOCKING ANNOUNCEMENT, MADE THIS STATEMENT.
VICTOR. YOU NEED TO EAT SOMETHING. YOU'VE BEEN STARING AT THAT ALL DAY.
PLEASE.
THANKS. BUT--I'M NOT HUNGRY.
WE DON'T KNOW WHAT KIND OF MISUNDERSTANDING OR PROVOCATION OUR ALIEN VISITOR WAS RESPONDING TO.
AS SOON AS WE CAN TALK TO THEM, I'M SURE WE CAN IRON THIS OUT AND HAVE A PEACEFUL CONVERSATION THAT WILL BENEFIT BOTH OUR VISITORS AND THE WHOLE HUMAN SPECIES.
CNN
I SHOULD HAVE HEARD FROM MY FAMILY BY NOW, IMALA.

THEY WERE HEADED TO WEIGH STATION FOUR TO WARN THEM. NOW THE NEWS IS SAYING THE STATION WAS DESTROYED.
MAYBE YOUR FAMILY GOT THEIR AFTERWARDS.

YOU DON'T KNOW MY FAMILY, IMALA.
EVEN IF THEY MISSED THE ALIEN SHIP, THEY WOULD'VE GONE AFTER IT TO TRY AND STOP IT.
FREE MINERS ARE STUBBORN THAT WAY.
THE KUIPER BELT IS IN CHAOS RIGHT NOW, VICTOR. NOT MANY TRANSMISSIONS ARE GETTING THROUGH.
LET'S WAIT AND HOPE FOR THE BEST.

HEY, YOU'RE NOT ALONE IN THIS.
YOU KNOW, FOR SOMEONE WHO'S SUPPOSED TO BE BAD WITH PEOPLE, YOU'RE DOING OKAY.
I KNOW. LOOK AT ME. PROGRESS.

"WE CONTINUE OUR LIVE SATELLITE COVERAGE OF THE ALIEN VESSEL, WHICH MOMENTS AGO MOVED INTO A GEOSYNCHRONOUS ORBIT AROUND EARTH.
"KENWE ZUBEKA, DIRECTOR OF ALIEN AFFAIRS FOR THE U.N., IS NOW APPROACHING THE VESSEL WITH GIFTS AND TOKENS OF PEACE FROM A HUNDRED AND EIGHTY-SEVEN COUNTRIES."
WELCOME. ON BEHALF OF THE PEOPLE OF EARTH, I EXTEND A HAND OF FELLOWSHIP TO YOU, OUR BRETHREN OF THE GALAX--

WE LOST THE NEWS FEED.
DID YOU SEE THAT? IT--IT WASTED THAT SHIP. IT JUST BLEW IT OUT OF THE SKY.
TRY ANOTHER STATION.
GUANGDONG PROVINCE, CHINA.
MAZER, DID YOU SEE THAT?
I SAW.
PATU, GET ME A SAT-LINK WITH NEW ZEALAND.
NO CAN DO, MATE. I CAN'T PICK UP A SIGNAL.
UM, MAZER.
AH, NUTS.

THOOOM
ARE YOU SEEING WHAT I'M SEEING?
IT'S SPINNING INTO THE GROUND, DIGGING IN. LIKE A FORTRESS.
WHOOSH
NOT GOOD. THIS IS DEFINITELY NOT GOOD.
THERE ARE PEOPLE DOWN THERE. REINHARDT, GET US IN THE AIR.

PATU. LET'S GO!
YEAH YEAH, KEEP YOUR SHIRT ON.
PLEASE TELL ME WE'RE GOING AWAY FROM THAT THING AND NOT TOWARD IT.
TOWARD IT.
THOUGHT SO.
BLAM
BOOM
BOOM
BOOM
GET US UP NOW!
ALL RIGHT, ALL RIGHT.
HOLD ON TO YOUR LUNCHES.

RED DRAGON. RED DRAGON. THIS IS LIEUTENANT MAZER RACKHAM OF THE NZ S.A.S. WE ARE TAKING FIRE. OVER.
THE CHINESE AIR FORCE WOULD BE NICE ABOUT NOW.
WORKING ON IT.
REPEAT: TAKING FIRE AT LATITUDE TWENTY-FOUR DEGREES, FORTY MINUTES, FIVE POINT SIXTY-THREE SECONDS.
LONGITUDE ONE HUNDRED TWELVE DEGREES--
MAYDAY. MAYDAY.
UHHNN!

PATU!
BLAM
BLAM
BLAM
BLAM
BOOM

GURU-eFX

"We were in the rice paddy, when they came. Their ships were small and fast, and they each carried ten of their kind. One ship landed light as a leaf near my son Jianyu. He did not run away. He thought it was wonderful. There was no fire or smoke, no loud noise. You could not see what was inside. The door opened. The creatures, those we now call the Kongbù, the Horror, they came out. I screamed for Jianyu across the field. I told him to run. The Kongbù sprayed a mist, and it kept spreading, like morning mist that creeps just above the ground. The mist reached Jianyu, and he dropped. I ran toward him, but my brother Minsheng grabbed my arm and pulled me away. The Kongbù sprayed their mist everywhere like we spray to kill the barnyard grass. They killed my wife Meilin. She had our baby Shihong in her arms. The Kongbù did not care. We are barnyard grass to them. I broke free of my brother and ran, but then the Kongbù began to tear the land away, and I was thrown back. When I woke, I ran to the place where Meilin had fallen. I found only blackness and ashes."

–Kwong Siyu, rice farmer, Guangdong Province, China. Excerpt from **Voices from the Fire: Rural Survivors of the Formic Invasion.**

RICE FIELDS, GUANGDONG PROVINCE, CHINA.
WHERE AM I?
STILL IN THE LAND OF THE LIVING, SOLDIER, THOUGH HELL CANNOT BE MUCH WORSE.
MY TEAM...
DO NOT GET UP. YOUR WOUNDS HAVE NOT YET HEALED.
DID NOT SURVIVE. YOU WOULD HAVE DIED WITH THEM IF MY GRANDSON HAD NOT BROUGHT YOU HERE WITH OUR MULE.
DRINK. IT TASTES LIKE GOAT DUNG, BUT IT WILL STRENGTHEN YOU.
WORSE THAN GOAT DUNG.
BUT THANK YOU.
I AM DANWAN. MY GRANDSON IS BINGWEN.
MAZER RACKHAM. NEW ZEALAND SPECIAL AIR SERVICE.

I HAVE TO WARN MY PEOPLE.
WHAT WARNING WILL YOU GIVE? THE WHOLE WORLD KNOWS THAT CHINA BURNS.
SEE FOR YOURSELF.
IT IS NOT FIRE THE INVADERS USE, BUT CHEMICALS. MISTS AND SEEDS OF DEATH.
SPRAYED HEAVILY, PLANTS AND ANIMALS DIE WITHIN HALF AN HOUR. LIGHT SPRAYING, AND THE LIVING THINGS WILT OVER TIME.
THEN THE INVADERS PEEL THE LAND AWAY LIKE A SKIN, TAKING EVERYTHING WITH THEM.

MY SON AND HIS WIFE WERE KILLED AND TAKEN IN THE FIELDS.
I HAVE NOT TOLD THE BOY, THOUGH I THINK HE SUSPECTS.
TAKEN WHERE?
THE LANDER. THERE IS A MOUNTAIN OF DEATH THERE. THOUSANDS OF PEOPLE. THOUSANDS OF ACRES OF VEGETATION. ALL PILED HIGH, ROTTING IN THE SUN.
I HEAR FIGHTERS.
THERE ARE MANY BATTLES IN THE SKY EVERY DAY.
"SOME OF THESE WE WIN.
"IN EVERY OTHER WAY, WE LOSE."

TRAINING FACILITY, MOBILE OPERATIONS POLICE, INDIA.
OUR REQUESTS TO ENTER CHINA HAVE BEEN DENIED. OUR ORDERS ARE TO HOLD OUR POSITION HERE.
AND DO WHAT? PLAY SOLITAIRE? CHINA NEEDS US.
THE CHINESE DON'T WANT A FOREIGN ARMY ON THEIR SOIL. EVEN A HELPFUL ONE.
THE RUSSIANS OFFERED, BUT THE CHINESE DON'T THINK THE RUSSIANS WOULD LEAVE WHEN IT'S OVER.
AMERICA IS HELPING IN THE AIR, BUT CHINA SAYS NO TROOPS.
THAT'S ASININE. THEIR PEOPLE ARE DYING.
EVERYTHING'S DYING. FORMICS ARE NOW DROPPING BACTERIA INTO THE OCEANS, KILLING ALL MARINE LIFE.
THEY'RE KILLING THE *WHALES*, TOO? THAT'S IT. NOW I'M ROYALLY PISSED.

CAPTAIN, WE'VE TRAINED FOR THIS.
NOBODY HAS TRAINED FOR THIS.
WE'RE BETTER PREPARED THAN ANYONE ELSE.
AGREED. THAT'S WHY I'M GOING.
I'LL HAVE TO CROSS THE BORDER ILLEGALLY. I'LL BE LABELED A DESERTER AND COURT-MARTIALED FOR DOING SO.
I CAN'T ASK THE SAME OF YOU.
YOU DON'T HAVE TO ASK. WE'RE COMING WITH YOU.
BETTER BELIEVE IT.
FAT CHANCE I'M STAYING HERE.
GOOD. I COULD USE THE HELP.

DOCKING BAY, MOON.
JUKE
YOU HAD THE FORMICS IN YOUR SIGHTS, LEM.
AND YOU HAD THE GRAVITY LASER. WHY DIDN'T YOU BLOODY USE IT?
IT'S NICE TO SEE YOU TOO, FATHER. AND NO, I'M NOT INJURED. THANKS FOR ASKING.
FORGIVE ME, SON. YOU'RE ALIVE. THAT'S ALL THAT MATTERS.
THE MEDIA WANTS TO TALK TO YOU. YOU'RE A HERO FOR LEADING THAT ASSAULT AGAINST THE FORMICS IN THE BELT.
I'M NO HERO, FATHER. NOR DID I LEAD THE ASSAULT.

YOU ARE WHAT THE MEDIA SAYS YOU ARE, LEM. WE WILL MAKE NO EFFORT TO CORRECT THEIR PERCEPTIONS.
IF THEY ASK, YOU RUSHED HOME BECAUSE YOU CARRY ON YOUR SHIP PROPRIETARY TECH FROM JUKE LIMITED THAT YOU BELIEVE CAN END THIS WAR.
I WILL NOT BECOME SOME PAWN IN YOUR WAR-PROFITEERING EFFORT, FATHER.
HOW DARE YOU. DO YOU THINK SO LITTLE OF ME?
DESPITE WHAT YOUR MOTHER MAY HAVE TOLD YOU, I AM NOT A SOULLESS MAN, LEM. THE MILITARY ARE IDIOTS. SPACE IS *OUR* FRONTIER. I OWN IT. AND WE'RE THE BEST EQUIPPED TO TAKE IT BACK.
YOU MURDERING PIRATE! YOU CLAIM JUMPER! YOU KILLED MARCO!
VICTOR, NO!

GET THIS ROCK RUSTLER AWAY FROM MY SON!
WHAT ABOUT MY FAMILY? WHAT ABOUT EL CAVADOR? YOU KILL THEM, TOO?
LET HIM GO.
EL CAVADOR WAS DESTROYED.

THE MEN ARE DEAD. CONCEPCION, TOO. THE WOMEN AND CHILDREN WERE PUT ON ANOTHER SHIP. I DON'T KNOW WHAT HAPPENED TO IT.
I'M SORRY.

CHINA.
DANWAN, YOU CAN'T STAY HERE. YOU MUST GO NORTH WITH THE OTHER FAMILIES.
THIS LAND HAS BEEN IN MY FAMILY FOR NINE GENERATIONS, MAZER. NOTHING AND NO ONE WILL TAKE IT FROM US.
I OWE YOU MY LIFE. BUT I MUST LEAVE AT FIRST LIGHT.
NO!
YOU CAN'T GO. YOU ARE ONE OF US NOW. YOU CAN STAY AND LIVE HERE, WITH US.
HUSH, BINGWEN.
REST, MAZER. YOU ARE NOT WELL ENOUGH TO TRAVEL, BUT I DO NOT THINK I CAN STOP YOU. I WILL KEEP WATCH.

AH!
PSSHH
GRANDFATHER!

SCHUKK!

BINGWEN, COVER YOUR MOUTH!

DON'T BREATHE THE MIST!

IT'S TOXIC!

LOOK OUT!

BOOOM

SPLOOSH!

SHUNKK!

AHHH!
BZZT!

GRANDFATHER.
BINGWEN, WE NEED TO MOVE. NOW. I'LL TAKE YOU TO ONE OF THE FAMILIES.

BUT I WANT TO STAY WITH *YOU.*
I CAN BE YOUR SON. I OBEY. I AM A GOOD SON.
YOU ARE NOT MY SON. AND WHERE I'M GOING CHILDREN CANNOT COME. GET YOUR THINGS.
BUT--WE CAN'T LEAVE GRANDFATHER TO BE PICKED BY THE BIRDS.

FWOOM

THIS FAMILY IS GOING NORTH. THEY'VE AGREED TO TAKE YOU. YOU'LL BE SAFE WITH THEM.
I'LL BE SAFER WITH YOU.
I AM GOING **TOWARD** DANGER, BINGWEN, NOT AWAY FROM IT.

TAKE THIS. YOUR GRANDFATHER WOULD WANT YOU TO HAVE IT.
AND DON'T FOLLOW ME. YOU WOULD ENDANGER BOTH OF US. I WILL NOT PROTECT YOU.

COME INTO THE LIGHT. I KNOW YOU'RE OUT THERE.
I TOLD YOU NOT TO FOLLOW ME, BINGWEN.
YOU NEED HELP. YOU'RE LOOKING FOR THE LANDER. I CAN TAKE YOU TO IT.
HERE. YOU'RE PROBABLY THIRSTY.
EASY, WATER HOG. THAT'S GOT TO LAST US.
DOES THIS MEAN I CAN COME WITH YOU?
GO TO SLEEP, BINGWEN. IT'S LATE.

WHAT IS ALL THIS STUFF?
PILOT'S GEAR. HE MUST HAVE EJECTED AND LANDED HERE.
YOU THINK HIS FRIENDS FOUND HIM?
SOMETHING FOUND HIM.

WHAT ARE YOU GOING TO DO WHEN YOU REACH THE LANDER, MAZER?
DESTROY IT.
HOW?
NO IDEA. I'M IMPROVISING.

BUT WE'VE GOT A PISTOL, A FUNKY ALIEN GUN WE DON'T KNOW HOW TO USE, AN OLD SWORD, BINOCULARS, AN OVERSIZED HELMET, AND SOME CHOPSTICKS.
SO I THINK THE ODDS ARE IN OUR FAVOR.

IT'S DECAY. THEY'RE BREAKING DOWN THE BIOMASS.
SPRAYING IT WITH SOME KIND OF MICROBE SOLUTION.

THIS PLACE STINKS.
WHY BREAK IT DOWN?
FOR FOOD OR FUEL, IS MY GUESS.
UM, MAZER.

GO GO GO!
VZZTT
BZZZT
BZZZT
AHH!
DON'T--
--MOVE,
BINGWEN.
BZZZT

BLAM
BLAM
BLAM
BLAM
BLAM
ROOOOM

SHHINK
GET IN THE VEHICLE! MOVE!

THIS PLACE WILL BE CRAWLING WITH BUGS IN FIFTEEN SECONDS.

NO ONE'S TAILING US, CAPTAIN. AND THE AIR IN HERE CHECKS OUT.
ALL RIGHT. MASKS OFF.
ARE YOU OUT OF YOUR MIND, MAZER? WALTZING INTO A HOT ZONE WITH A CLOTH OVER YOUR FACE? AND WITH A CHILD, NO LESS. THAT'S NINE WAYS OF STUPID.
CAPTAIN O'TOOLE? THE MOPS ARE IN CHINA?
NOT OFFICIALLY. CALL US CONCERNED CITIZENS OF THE WORLD. WE'RE DOWN TO EIGHTEEN MEN.
THE ONLY OTHER TROOPS NEARBY ARE A FEW THOUSAND DEAD CHINESE MARINES TO THE EAST. THE CHINESE KEEP SENDING THEM, AND THE FORMICS KEEP MOWING THEM DOWN.
FORMICS? THAT'S WHAT WE'RE CALLING THEM?
I HAVE OTHER NAMES. NONE OF WHICH I'LL REPEAT IN FRONT OF A CHILD.
THIS CHILD HAS A NAME, YOU KNOW.

WE NEED TO TAKE OUT THAT LANDER.
EASIER SAID. A FRONTAL ASSAULT'S SUICIDE. AND THE CHINESE HAVE ALREADY TRIED BOMBING IT. IT'S SHIELDED.
I WAS TRAINING WITH THE CHINESE BEFORE THIS WENT DOWN. ASSUMING IT'S STILL STANDING, THERE'S A WEAPONS CACHE WEST OF HERE. I MAY HAVE AN IDEA.
WHAT THE DEVIL IS THAT?
SK
THAT, CAPTAIN, IS HOW WE ARE GOING TO WIN THIS WAR.

TAN 11
GURU-eFX

United States Air Force Communiqué

HIGHLY CONFIDENTIAL

DATE: <redacted>
TO: Secretary of Defense
SUBJECT: Code Name ORBIT BULLY

Mr. Secretary,
Our coordinated attack against the Formic ship in geosynchronous orbit at 0700 this morning D.C. time resulted in no visible damage to the alien vessel.

Fifty-four warheads were fired from sixteen different positions, and all warheads hit their target. However, as the embedded video file named <redacted> will show, all warheads struck what appears to be a shield surrounding the Formic vessel.

Repeated attempts to destabilize this shield using <redacted> and <redacted> failed.

Our balls are in a vice, Mr. Secretary. We're like flies swatting at a <redacted> bowling ball.

Respectfully,
General Max Chaykin
US Air Force Earth Orbit Division
Rangor Space Station

THE MOON.
Join Today
UN
United Nation's Peacekeepers
I'M SORRY, MR. DELGADO. WE CAN'T ACCEPT YOU.
WHY NOT?
YOU'RE NOT A CITIZEN OF ANY COUNTRY. EVERY SOLDIER IN OUR FORCES MUST REPRESENT A NATION. YOU WERE BORN IN SPACE.
UN
WHAT DIFFERENCE DOES *THAT* MAKE? PEOPLE ON EARTH ARE DYING. YOU THINK THEY CARE IF THEIR RESCUERS HAVE A BIRTH CERTIFICATE?

SORRY. THAT'S OUR POLICY.
YOU'LL LET THE WORLD BE DESTROYED BECAUSE OF A *POLICY?*
WITH ALL DUE RESPECT, MR. DELGADO, ONE PERSON CAN'T MAKE THAT MUCH DIFFERENCE.
WITH ALL DUE RESPECT, MR. RECRUITER GUY, YOU'RE WRONG.

LUNAR TRADE DEPARTMENT.
UNBELIEVABLE.
MORE STUPID RULES AND RED TAPE. HOW DO PLANET-SIDE PEOPLE GET ANYTHING DONE?
I COULDN'T AGREE MORE.
HELLO, VICTOR.
WHAT IS HE DOING HERE?
BEFORE YOU GO SUPERNOVA, HEAR HIM OUT.
HE FOUND YOUR MOTHER.

THE WU-HU SHIP CARRYING YOUR MOTHER AND THE OTHER WOMEN FROM EL CAVADOR DOCKED AT THIS ASTEROID IN THE BELT.
WHEN'S IT COMING HERE?
IT ISN'T.
WU-HU CORP HAS STOPPED ALL SHIPMENTS TO THE MOON UNTIL THE PROBLEM WITH THE FORMICS IS OVER.
PROBLEM?
I THINK THE POSSIBLE EXTINCTION OF THE HUMAN RACE IS MORE THAN A ***PROBLEM.***
HE'S TRYING TO HELP, VICTOR.
HIMSELF, MAYBE.
I DON'T BLAME YOU FOR HATING ME, VICTOR. BUT I'M TRYING TO MAKE THINGS RIGHT.
THAT'S WHY I'M MEETING WITH IMALA. MY FATHER ASKED ME TO CORRECT THE COMPANY'S DISCREPANCIES WITH THE LUNAR TRADE DEPARTMENT.

DISCREPANCIES? THE WORLD IS ABOUT TO END AND YOU TWO WANT TO CLEAR UP SOME TRADE VIOLATIONS AND BACK TAXES?
MY FATHER BELIEVES HE CAN END THIS WAR, VICTOR.
BY HELPING HIM HERE AND ALLOWING HIM TO FOCUS ON THE WAR EFFORT, *I'M*, IN ESSENCE, HELPING THE WAR EFFORT, TOO. AND SO IS IMALA.
I'M GIVING HIM A COPY OF MY FILES, VICTOR. THAT'S ALL.
IF UKKO WANTS TO COME CLEAN, I'M NOT GOING TO STOP HIM BY WITHHOLDING WHAT I'VE FOUND.
THIS IS A GOOD THING.
YEAH. PEACHY. I'M HAPPY FOR YOU.

JUKE PRODUCTION FACILITY.
WHY AREN'T THE DRONES READY?
OUR GUYS ARE WORKING AROUND THE CLOCK, MR. JUKES.
THE HOLDUP IS THE GRAVITY LASERS. WE'RE RETROFITTING THEM ONTO THE DRONES LIKE YOU ASKED, BUT WE CAN'T BUILD THE LASERS FAST ENOUGH.
IS THAT SO?
THEN LET ME ASK YOU THIS, MR. BULLICK, HAVE YOU EVER HAD ALL YOUR CELL WALLS BREAK DOWN?
UM... WHAT?
THE FORMICS CARRY THESE DEFOLIANTS THAT THEY SPRAY INTO PEOPLE'S FACES THAT BREAK DOWN CELLULAR WALLS.
THINK OF IT AS A LIQUEFYING DEATH RAY.
ONE SPRAY TO THE FACE AND YOU'RE A PUDDLE OF BLOODY GOO.
YOU FOLLOW?

SO UNLESS YOU WANT TO BE A LIQUID, MR. BULLICK, I SUGGEST YOU PUT YOUR TAIL IN GEAR.
BECAUSE WE'RE IT.
THE MILITARY ARE IDIOTS. NOTHING THEY THROW AT THE ALIEN SHIP IS GETTING THROUGH. NOT CONVENTIONAL MISSILES. NOT WEAPONIZED SHUTTLES. ZILCH.
OUR ONLY HOPE, AS FAR AS I'M CONCERNED, IS THE GRAVITY LASER. IT HAS THE BEST CHANCE OF PENETRATING THE FORMIC SHIELDS.
AM I MAKING MYSELF CLEAR, MR. BULLICK? AM I GETTING THROUGH THAT HARD HAT OF YOURS?
YES, SIR.
SPLENDID.
NOW GET BACK TO WORK.

MOON DOCK.
GOING SOMEWHERE?
WHY DO YOU ASK? SO YOU CAN PASS THAT INFO ON TO LEM JUKES?
YOU'RE NOT BEING FAIR, VICTOR.
YOU CAN'T TRUST HIM, IMALA. HE'S A CORPORATE. A MURDERER.
SO, NOW YOU'RE LEAVING?
MY FAMILY BREACHED THE HULL OF THAT SHIP.
THEY MADE MORE OF A DENT WITH A DOZEN FREE MINERS THAN THE WHOLE ARMADA HAS. YET EVERYONE IS IGNORING *HOW* THEY DID IT.
SO YOU'RE GOING TO LAUNCH YOURSELF AT THE FORMICS? ALONE? THAT'S IMPOSSIBLE.
I'M A FREE MINER, IMALA. WE DON'T BELIEVE IN *IMPOSSIBLE.*

AND WHEN YOU LAND ON THEIR SHIP? THEN WHAT? YOU'LL KNOCK AND ASK THEM TO LEAVE?
NO. I'LL CUT A HOLE, GO INSIDE, AND BLOW IT UP.
CUT IT OPEN WITH WHAT?
I'LL BUILD SOMETHING. THERE ARE PLENTY OF SCRAP PARTS OUT FLOATING AROUND EARTH.
YOU MEAN SPACE JUNK?
THIS IS HOW WE SURVIVED AS FREE MINERS, IMALA. WE MADE DO WITH WHAT WE HAD. OUR LIVES DEPENDED ON IT.
I'M COMING WITH YOU.
NO WAY.
YES WAY. YOU'RE STILL UNDER MY SUPERVISION AS AN UNDOCUMENTED ALIEN. ARGUE WITH ME, AND I'LL HAVE YOU ARRESTED.

CHINA.
THE DRILL-SKI WORKS LIKE AN EARTHWORM. IT SCRAPES UP EARTH AND ROCK IN THE FRONT AND EJECTS IT OUT THE BACK.
BUT THE EJECTA IS SUPERHOT. DIG THROUGH ROCK, AND IT SPEWS BACK LAVA. YOU DO NOT WANT TO BE FOLLOWING ONE OF THESE BAD BOYS.
SK

HENCE THE COOL SUITS. WHEN YOU PUNCH THROUGH ROCK, YOU START MOVING FAST AND EVERYTHING GETS SUPERHOT.
EVEN THE AIR. WITHOUT THE COOL SUIT, YOU'D BE BONES AND ASHES.

LOVELY. SOUNDS LIKE A THEME PARK RIDE IN HELL.

SO WHAT'S THE PLAN, CAPTAIN? DIGGING A HOLE DOESN'T SOUND LIKE A STRATEGY.
THE LANDER IS IMPENETRABLE. NOTHING HAS CRACKED IT. BOMBS, TANKS. IT'S LIKE THEIR SHIP IN SPACE. TOTALLY SHIELDED.
SO WE'RE GOING UNDER THE SHIELD.
THREE DRILL-SKIS WILL GO IN HOT STRAIGHT UP INTO THE BOTTOM OF THE LANDER USING THE BIT-NOSE. ME, MAZER, AND DEEN.
DEEN WILL BE CARRYING A TACTICAL NUKE.
ONCE THE DRILL-SKIS ARE IN, WE'LL DITCH DEEN'S BOMB-SKI INSIDE. HE'LL THEN CLIMB INTO MY DRILL-SKI, AND WE'LL ALL DIVE, NOSHING THROUGH BEDROCK.
THEN KA-BOOM.
ANY QUESTIONS?

SANTA'S PAJAMAS! THIS SUIT IS COLD. WHY DIDN'T YOU TELL ME TO WEAR EIGHT PAIRS OF UNDERWEAR?
I WON'T BE ABLE TO HAVE CHILDREN EITHER.
LOOK ON THE BRIGHT SIDE, DEEN. YOU WON'T FALL ASLEEP AT THE WHEEL.
LET'S MOVE, GENTLEMEN.
MAZER, WHAT'S OUR DISTANCE?

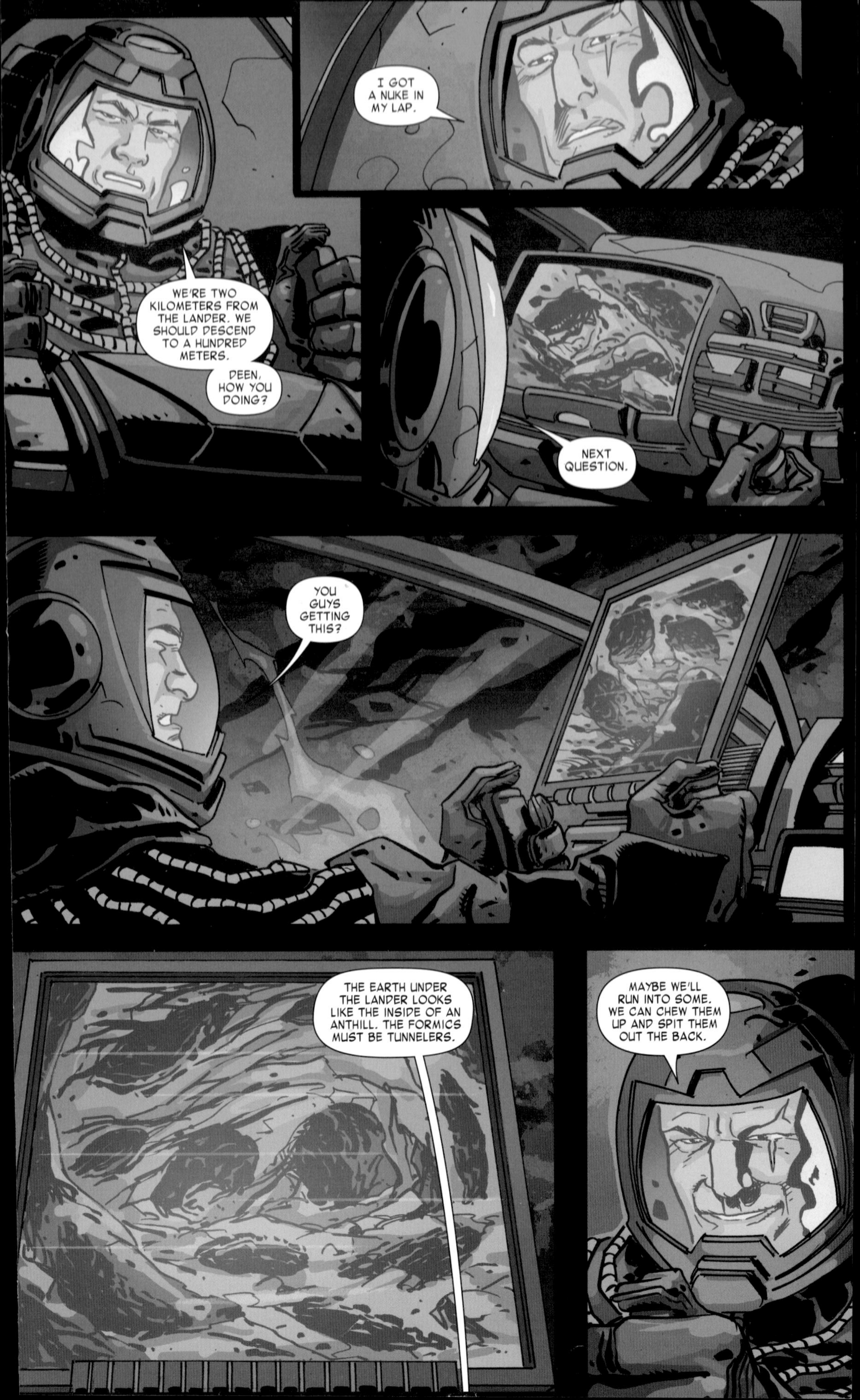
I GOT A NUKE IN MY LAP.
WE'RE TWO KILOMETERS FROM THE LANDER. WE SHOULD DESCEND TO A HUNDRED METERS.
DEEN, HOW YOU DOING?
NEXT QUESTION.
YOU GUYS GETTING THIS?
THE EARTH UNDER THE LANDER LOOKS LIKE THE INSIDE OF AN ANTHILL. THE FORMICS MUST BE TUNNELERS.
MAYBE WE'LL RUN INTO SOME. WE CAN CHEW THEM UP AND SPIT THEM OUT THE BACK.

WE'RE DIRECTLY BELOW THE LANDER, CAPTAIN. YOU GIVE THE WORD.
PUNCH IT.
WAIT. PULL UP. THERE'S AN AIR POCKET AHEAD.

WELL THAT WAS ANTICLIMACTIC.
WE COULD FLY UP THERE WITH ENOUGH EJECTA BEHIND US, BUT WE'D NEVER GET A GRIP ON THE HULL. WE'D BOUNCE OFF.
NOW WHAT, CAPTAIN?
WE IMPROVISE.
MAZER, COULD WE BURN OUR WAY IN? WHAT 'F WE TURN THESE GOPHERS AROUND AND HIT THE UNDERSIDE OF THE LANDER WITH OUR LAVA SPEW?
COULD WE MELT A HOLE BIG ENOUGH FOR DEEN TO LAUNCH THROUGH?
MAYBE. TROUBLE S, THE DRILL-SKIS 'EREN'T DESIGNED FOR STRAIGHT IVES COMPLETELY NOSE DOWN.
WE'LL HAVE TO GET OUT AND POSITION THE DRILL-SKIS UPRIGHT MANUALLY WITH THE STILTS.
DEEN, GO DEEP. MAZER AND I WILL MELT A HOLE.
AFTER YOU LAUNCH UP INTO IT, WE'LL COME UP AFTER YOU. THEN WE DITCH THE NUKE AS PLANNED.
SOUNDS DANGEROUS. I'M IN.

LATER:

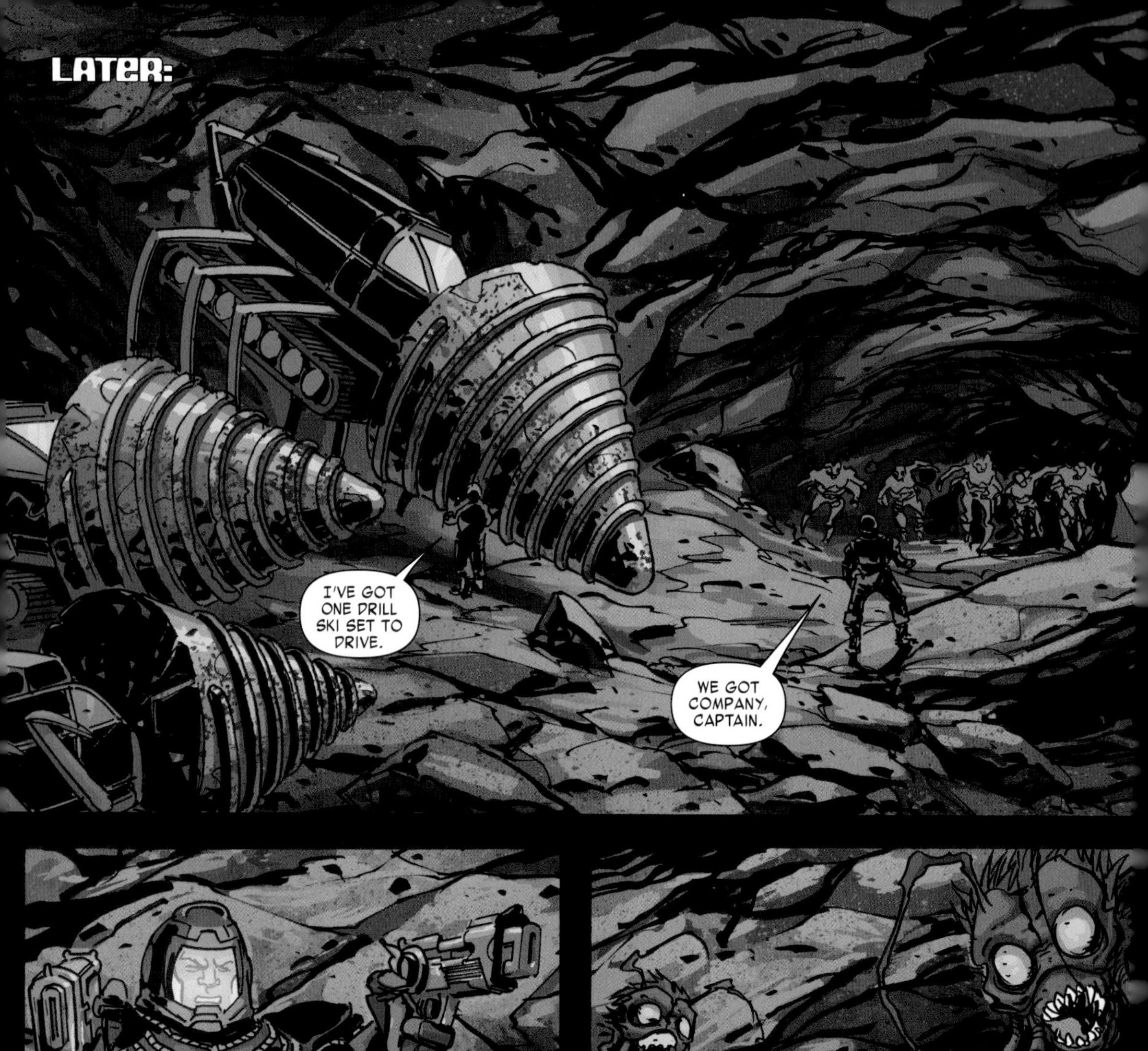
I'VE GOT ONE DRILL SKI SET TO DRIVE.
WE GOT COMPANY, CAPTAIN.

HOLD THEM OFF WHILE I RAISE THE OTHER ONE.

HAPPY TO.

MIGHT WANT TO HURRY UP. THESE WERE JUST THE SCOUTS.
THE SWARM COMES NEXT.

IT'S ABOUT TO GET REAL CROWDED IN HERE, CAPTAIN.
DEEN. ABORT.
WE GOT A SWARM OF UNFRIENDLIES UP HERE. YOU WOULDN'T BE ABLE TO GET OUT OF YOUR DRILL-SKI AND INTO MINE WITHOUT BEING OVERRUN.
IF WE LEAVE, CAPTAIN, THEY'LL SHIELD THE UNDERSIDE OF THAT LANDER.
IT'S NOW OR NEVER.

MAZER, TAKE THE DRILL-SKI AND BURN THE HOLE. I'LL STAY AND RETRIEVE DEEN.
HOW?
THAT'S MY PROBLEM. MOVE!
THIS IS COMPLETELY INSANE.
AND YOUR POINT IS?
I'M SPEWING. I'VE GOT MY TRACKS IN REVERSE TO KEEP ME FROM DIVING, BUT I DON'T KNOW HOW LONG I CAN HOLD IT.
MAZER, GET THAT LAVA HIGHER!
I'M TRYING! IT'S NOT EXACTLY EASY TO AIM!
DEEN, WE'VE BREECHED THE HULL. PUNCH IT.
ROGER THAT.
HERE I COME, LADIES.
THAT HOLE BETTER BE BIG ENOUGH.

KABOOM
CRASH
UHHH... BOY. THAT HURT.
DEEN. STATUS.
THE LANDING WAS A LITTLE OFF, CAPTAIN. I'D GIVE IT AN EIGHT POINT FIVE.

GET READY TO SWITCH TO MY DRILL-SKI, I'M COMING UP.
DON'T BOTHER. SHOW'S OVER, CAPTAIN. TIME FOR YOU TO SKEDADDLE.
NOT WITHOUT YOU, I'M NOT!
00.30
TOO LATE. I'VE ALREADY STARTED THE CLOCK.
NEGATIVE! I AM COMING FOR YOU! STOP THE COUNTDOWN! THAT'S AN ORDER!
DON'T BE STUPID. THERE'S NO WAY YOU CAN RETRIEVE ME. I KNEW THAT BEFORE I GOT HERE.
JUST MAKE SURE WE WIN, EH?
MAKE IT QUICK, UGLY.

COME ON.
GET DEEP. GET DEEP.

WELCOME, CAPTAIN O'TOOLE.
ON BEHALF OF THE CHINESE ARMY, THANK YOU FOR DESTROYING THE LANDER.
ALSO--

--YOU'RE UNDER ARREST.

AS I WAS JUST TELLING LIEUTENANT RACKHAM HERE--
CHARGES INCLUDE, ILLEGALLY CROSSING OUR BORDERS, STEALING MILITARY PROPERTY, AND CONDUCTING A NUCLEAR STRIKE ON CHINESE SOIL.
WE JUST DESTROYED THE GUYS WHO HAVE BEEN SLAUGHTERING YOUR PEOPLE.
YOU'RE SUPPOSED TO SEE WHAT WE DID AND COPY IT.
WE WILL.
BUT YOU ARE ALSO ARRESTED. IN CHINA, MOST HEROES ARE ARRESTED FIRST. WE'RE USED TO IT.
NOW, COME WITH ME, GENTLEMEN.
"YOU MAY HAVE SCORED A VICTORY--
"--BUT THIS WAR IS FAR FROM OVER."

S E V E N

Official transcript of interview.
The People's Liberation Army File #: 342078-MR
Guangdong, China.

INTERVIEWER: State your name and age for the recorder please.
BINGWEN: Shi Bingwen. Eight years old.
INTERVIEWER: Lieutenant Mazer Rackham was hurt and unconscious when you found him. How did you get him home?
BINGWEN: My mule carried him.
INTERVIEWER: You lifted him onto your mule?
BINGWEN: I rigged a thing with rope and bamboo so he wasn't so heavy.
INTERVIEWER: Can you draw what you built on this pad here?

[subject draws]

INTERVIEWER: Where did you learn to build this?
BINGWEN: On our rice farm.
INTERVIEWER: Why did you help Lieutenant Rackham?
BINGWEN: If I saved him then maybe he would stay and protect us.
INTERVIEWER: But he didn't stay.
BINGWEN: No, he had to destroy the lander.
INTERVIEWER: And you went with him.
BINGWEN: If I'm old enough to die, I'm old enough to fight to stay alive.

HOW CAN PEOPLE BE SO WASTEFUL, IMALA?
LOOK AT THIS STUFF. WHY WOULD YOU THROW ANY OF THIS AWAY?
IT'S SPACE JUNK, VICTOR. NONE OF IT WORKS ANYMORE.
SO? ANYTHING CAN BE REPAIRED.
BY YOU MAYBE.
I JUST DON'T SEE WHY EVERYONE ISN'T OUT HERE SCOOPING ALL THIS UP.
BECAUSE GETTING HERE FROM THE SURFACE OF EARTH OR THE MOON COSTS MORE IN FUEL THAN THE VALUE OF THIS JUNK.
NOW GRAB WHAT YOU NEED, SO I CAN GET THIS SHUTTLE BACK.

WHAT CAN YOU POSSIBLY BUILD WITH THIS JUNK?
WELL THAT'S JUST IT. I'M GOING TO BUILD A BIG MOUND OF JUNK.
I'M SURE THAT'S A BRILLIANT IDEA SOMEHOW. I'M JUST NOT SEEING IT.
LOOK AT THE FORMIC SHIP OUT THERE, IMALA. IT'S SURROUNDED BY WRECKAGE.
"MILITARIES KEEP SENDING WAVE AFTER WAVE OF SHIPS. BUT THE FORMIC PROXIMITY DETECTORS DESTROY ANYTHING THAT MOVES."
SO NATURALLY A PILE OF JUNK IS THE ANSWER.
SORRY. STILL LOST HERE.
CAMOUFLAGE, IMALA.
I'LL DISGUISE MY TUG TO LOOK LIKE WRECKAGE. THEN I CAN FLOAT VERY, VERY SLOWLY RIGHT UP TO THE SHIP WITHOUT SETTING OFF ALARMS.
THAT ACTUALLY MAKES SENSE.
TRY NOT TO LOOK SO SURPRISED.

CHINA.
GENERAL SIMA, I PRESENT CAPTAIN WIT O'TOOLE OF THE MOBILE OPERATIONS POLICE--
--AND LIEUTENANT MAZER RACKHAM OF THE NEW ZEALAND SPECIAL AIR SERVICE.
WELCOME TO OUR LITTLE HOLE IN THE GROUND, GENTLEMEN. WE ARE FEW, BUT WE ARE ALIVE.
YOU ORDERED OUR ARREST?
YOU DETONATED A NUCLEAR BOMB ON CHINESE SOIL. THE GOVERNMENT FROWNS ON THAT.
WE'RE HELPING STOP THE SLAUGHTER OF YOUR PEOPLE.
DON'T THINK ME UNGRATEFUL, CAPTAIN O'TOOLE. BUT THE LAW IS THE LAW.

SO WE'RE PRISONERS NOW?
I CAN'T AFFORD THE MEN OR EQUIPMENT TO EXTRADITE YOU. WE'RE IN THE MIDDLE OF A WAR.
WE DON'T WANT TO LEAVE, GENERAL. WE WANT TO HELP.
WE'RE HOPING YOU'LL COPY WHAT WE DID AND DESTROY THE OTHER LANDERS.
ALREADY DOING THAT, CAPTAIN. I HAVE DRILL-SKI TEAMS ATTACKING THE LANDERS AS WE SPEAK.
I'M PLEASED TO HEAR YOU WANT TO HELP.
THE CHINESE MILITARY CAN LEARN MUCH FROM MEN WITH YOUR SKILLS, TRAINING, AND COURAGE.
HOWEVER--
--THERE IS THE ISSUE OF YOUR COURT-MARTIAL.

HE CAN'T BE SERIOUS.
WE DON'T HAVE *TIME* FOR THAT, GENERAL.
ACTUALLY WE DO. THE COURT-MARTIAL IS ALREADY OVER.
I JUST CONDUCTED IT WHILE WE WERE WALKING.
YOU'RE BOTH GUILTY.
I SENTENCE YOU TO LEAVE CHINESE SOIL.
YOU JUST SAID YOU COULDN'T EXTRADITE US.
TRUE. BUT I HAVE ANOTHER WAY TO GET YOU OFF CHINESE SOIL.
只有經授权的
IDENTITY CONFIRMED. ACCESS GRANTED.

HOW WOULD YOU LIKE TO TAKE THE FIGHT DIRECTLY TO THE MOTHER SHIP?
1002 LL
YOU WANT TO SEND US UP?
YOU'RE JOKING.
BELIEVE ME, LIEUTENANT RACKHAM, IF THERE'S ONE THING WE DON'T HAVE IN THE CHINESE MILITARY, IT'S A SENSE OF HUMOR.
COME, GENTLEMEN. YOUR COMPANIONS ARE WAITING.

THEY ARRESTED YOU TOO, HUH?
WE DIDN'T PUT UP A FIGHT. IT WOULD'VE ENDED IN CASUALTIES.
YEAH. THEIRS.
MAZER!

THEY SAID I CAN'T STAY WITH YOU.
THEY'RE GOING TO TAKE YOU SOMEWHERE SAFE, BINGWEN.

LET'S GO, BINGWEN. YOU'VE SEEN THE LIEUTENANT AS PROMISED. TIME TO SAY GOODBYE.

HE'S A SHARP KID. HE SHOULDN'T BE FORGOTTEN.
OH, HE WON'T BE. BELIEVE ME. YOU'VE ALREADY HALF-TRAINED HIM FOR US. VERY USEFUL.

EASIER TO TRAIN KIDS FOR WAR AND COMMAND THAN ADULTS-- FEWER BAD HABITS TO OVERCOME.
CHILD COMMANDERS? THAT'LL BE THE DAY.
DON'T KNOCK IT. I'D RATHER SERVE UNDER THAT KID THAN MOST OF THE COMMANDING OFFICERS I'VE HAD.

MOON DOCK.
HEY VICTOR, YOU GOT A MINUTE?
WHAT IS HE DOING HERE?
HE WANTS TO HELP.
YOU TOLD HIM WHAT I WAS DOING?
I THOUGHT I COULD TRUST YOU. I THOUGHT WE WERE FRIENDS.
HE HAS RESOURCES WE NEED, VICTOR.
YOU WANT TO DO ME A REAL FAVOR? TELL PRETTY BOY HERE TO GO EXPLORE A BLACK HOLE.

YOUR IDEA IS A GOOD ONE, VICTOR. BUT ONE TUG ISN'T ENOUGH. IF YOU LET ME SHARE THIS IDEA WITH MY FATHER--
WHY?
SO YOU CAN KILL MORE INNOCENT PEOPLE? STEAMROLL MORE FREE MINERS?
NO. SO WE CAN SAVE THE HUMAN RACE.
THINK, VICTOR. GETTING TO THE FORMIC SHIP IS ONE THING. DESTROYING IT IS QUITE ANOTHER.
YOUR FAMILY TRIED AND THEY FAILED. IF YOU THINK YOU CAN JUST SHOW UP AND WING IT, YOU'RE DEAD WRONG.
NOW TELL ME WHAT YOU NEED.
ALL RIGHT.
YOU BETTER WRITE THIS DOWN.

JUKE PRODUCTION FACILITY.
THAT'S A STUPID IDEA.
WHY WOULD I DISGUISE A FLEET OF DRONES AS DEBRIS? IT'S A FLEET. IT CAN'T SNEAK UP ON ANYTHING, CAMOUFLAGED OR NOT.
I'M NOT SUGGESTING YOU DISGUISE THE ENTIRE FLEET, FATHER.
I'M SUGGESTING YOU MAY NOT NEED A WHOLE FLEET.
THREE MEN ON EARTH JUST DESTROYED ONE OF THE FORMIC LANDERS.
THREE MEN.
A LITTLE THING CALLED A NUCLEAR BOMB HELPED IN THAT EFFORT, LEM. I WATCH THE NEWS.
MY POINT IS, HUGE FRONTAL ASSAULTS AREN'T WORKING.
A SMALL STRIKE TEAM MIGHT BE BEST.

HEAR THIS KID OUT, FATHER. HE HAS OTHER IDEAS THAT MIGHT HELP.
LOOK AROUND YOU, LEM.
I HAVE THE BRIGHTEST MINDS IN THE SOLAR SYSTEM ON MY PAYROLL. WHY WOULD I WASTE A SECOND OF MY TIME ON AN UNEDUCATED GRAVEL DIGGER?
FINE. THEN ARM HIS TUG WITH A GRAVITY LASER. THAT WOULD GIVE US VALUABLE INTEL.
WE'D KNOW HOW EFFECTIVE IT IS AGAINST THEIR SHIP.
OH, THAT'S GENIUS, LEM.
GIVE OUR MOST VALUABLE PROPRIETARY TECHNOLOGY TO SOMEONE WHO COULD EASILY SELL IT TO OUR COMPETITORS.
THAT'S BRILLIANT.
MR. JUKES, THE FORMIC SHIP APPEARS TO BE OPENING, SIR.

WHAT ARE THOSE?
ZOOM IN ON ONE OF THOSE SHIPS.
YES, SIR.
REINFORCEMENTS.
THERE'S GOT TO BE OVER A HUNDRED SHIPS.
GET AN EMERGENCY LASERLINE TO STASA AND THE UN. TELL THEM THEY'VE GOT HELL COMING.

GUANGZHOU, CHINA.

BLAM
BLAM
BLAM
BLAM
BLAM
BLAM

MOON.
YOU'RE NOT COMING, IMALA.
THE SHIP SEATS ONE PERSON COMFORTABLY.
YOU KNOW, MOST GUYS WOULDN'T MIND BEING STUCK IN A CRAMPED SPACE WITH ME.
THIS ISN'T A GAME, IMALA.
YOU THINK I DON'T KNOW WHAT'S AT STAKE?
I HAVE A FAMILY TOO, VICTOR. AND THEY'RE DOWN ON EARTH WHERE MILLIONS OF PEOPLE ARE DYING.
AND IF THERE'S ANYTHING I CAN DO TO HELP STOP THAT, ANYTHING AT ALL, I AM GOING TO DO IT.
BETTER LISTEN, VICTOR.
IT NEVER PAYS TO ARGUE WITH A WOMAN WHO'S SMARTER THAN YOU.

HERE'S EVERYTHING YOU ASKED FOR.
I DON'T SUPPOSE YOU THREW IN SOME NUKES FOR GOOD MEASURE.
SORRY. FRESH OUT.
BUT WHAT EXPLOSIVES I COULD GET, I GOT.
MOSTLY BY ILLEGAL MEANS.
I'M NOT SURE WHICH IS HARDER, GOING OFF TO KILL ALIENS OR THANKING YOU.
I'LL SPARE YOU HALF YOUR PAIN. NO THANKS NEEDED.
BUT BE QUICK. MY FATHER INTENDS TO LAUNCH HIS DRONES IN FIVE DAYS.
WHATEVER YOU PLAN TO DO, DO IT BEFORE THEN.
JUST BECAUSE WE'RE LYING CLOSE DOESN'T GIVE YOU THE RIGHT TO "ACCIDENTLY" BRUSH UP AGAINST ME, PAL.
WOULDN'T DREAM OF IT, IMALA. YOU'D BREAK MY FINGERS.

IF THEY PUT ME ON THAT CENTRIFUGE ONE MORE TIME, I'M GOING TO TOSS MY COOKIES.
I STILL DON'T GET IT, CAPTAIN. WHY ARE THE CHINESE TRAINING US TO BE ASTRONAUTS?
YEAH, WHY NOT SEND UP THEIR OWN PEOPLE?
BECAUSE THEY EXPECT US TO FAIL, GENTLEMEN.
CHINA. UNDERGROUND.
WE'RE GUINEA PIGS. THEY INTEND TO LEARN FROM OUR MISTAKES, COME IN AFTER US, AND WIN.
BUT WE'LL SURPRISE THEM.
WE WON'T FAIL. WE'LL END THIS WAR.
BUT ONLY IF WE STAY ALERT AND NOT ALLOW OURSELVES TO GET COMPLACENT. THIS FACILITY MAY BE WELL HIDDEN AND WELL GUARDED.
"BUT THAT CAN CHANGE IN AN INSTANT."

FORMICS. INSIDE. SPRAYING A GAS. OUR MASKS DON'T STOP IT.
WHAT DO WE DO?
WE GET THE HELL OUT. NOW!
BAM BAM BAM BAM
MOVE UPWIND! DON'T STOP RUNNING!

NOW WE DRIFT IN REAL SLOW.
AS LONG AS THEY CAN'T DETECT OUR HEAT SIGNATURES WE'RE FINE.
YOU MEAN THAT'S POSSIBLE?
THEY CAN TRAVEL AT NEAR LIGHTSPEED, IMALA. WHO KNOWS WHAT THEY CAN DO?
IT WOULD'VE BEEN NICE TO KNOW THAT BEFORE WE SET OUT.
IF YOU WAIT UNTIL YOU KNOW EVERYTHING, YOU NEVER DO ANYTHING.
WHO ARE YOU QUOTING? BEN FRANKLIN? SUN-TZU?
MY FATHER.
OKAY, I'M ON.
KEEP WATCH. IF I'M NOT BACK IN TWO HOURS, DRIFT AWAY WITHOUT ME.

MOON.
YOU CAN'T ATTACK TODAY, FATHER.
THERE'S NO POINT STICKING TO THE OLD SCHEDULE, LEM. THE FORMICS ARE GASSING ASIA.
I HAVE TWO PEOPLE MAKING A RUN ON THE MOTHER SHIP. YOU'LL KILL THEM IF YOU ATTACK NOW.
TWO PEOPLE?
EVERY MINUTE WE SPEND RUNNING OUR MOUTHS, *THOUSANDS* OF PEOPLE ARE DYING, LEM. BABIES, CHILDREN, WOMEN.
THEIR SKIN IS MELTING OFF THEIR BONES. AND YOU WANT ME TO LET THAT HAPPEN SO *TWO* OF YOUR PALS CAN PLAY COMMANDO?
NO. I WANT YOU TO HAVE FAITH IN AN IDEA THAT'S NOT YOUR OWN. FOR ONCE IN YOUR LIFE.
LAUNCH THE DRONES.

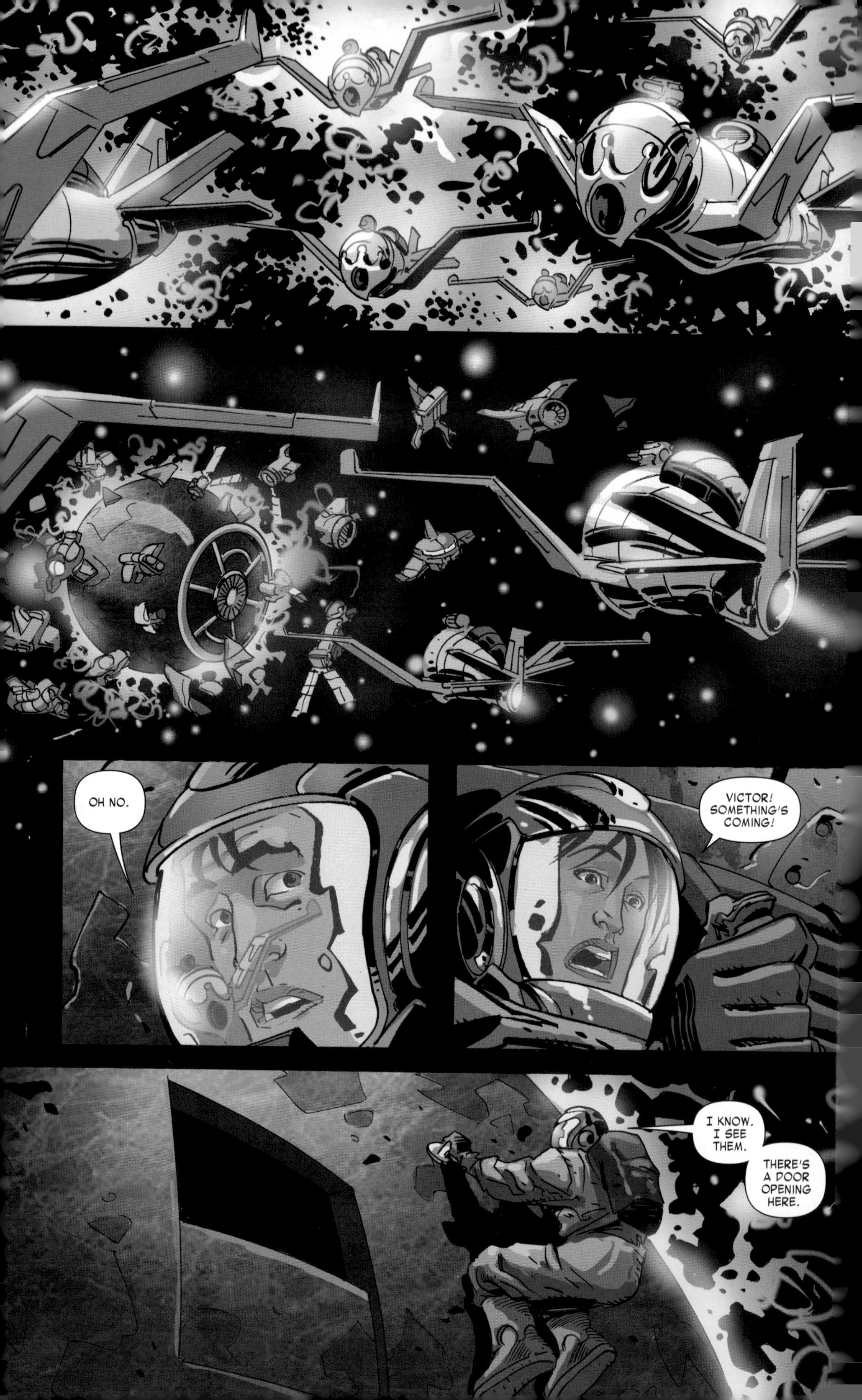
OH NO.
VICTOR! SOMETHING'S COMING!
I KNOW. I SEE THEM.
THERE'S A DOOR OPENING HERE.

TO BE CONTINUED...

#1 VARIANT BY BRYAN

ITCH & PAUL MOUNTS

CHARACTER DESIGNS BY GIANCARLO CARACUZZO

1
2
3
LEM'S SHIP

LEM JUKES

CONCEPCION

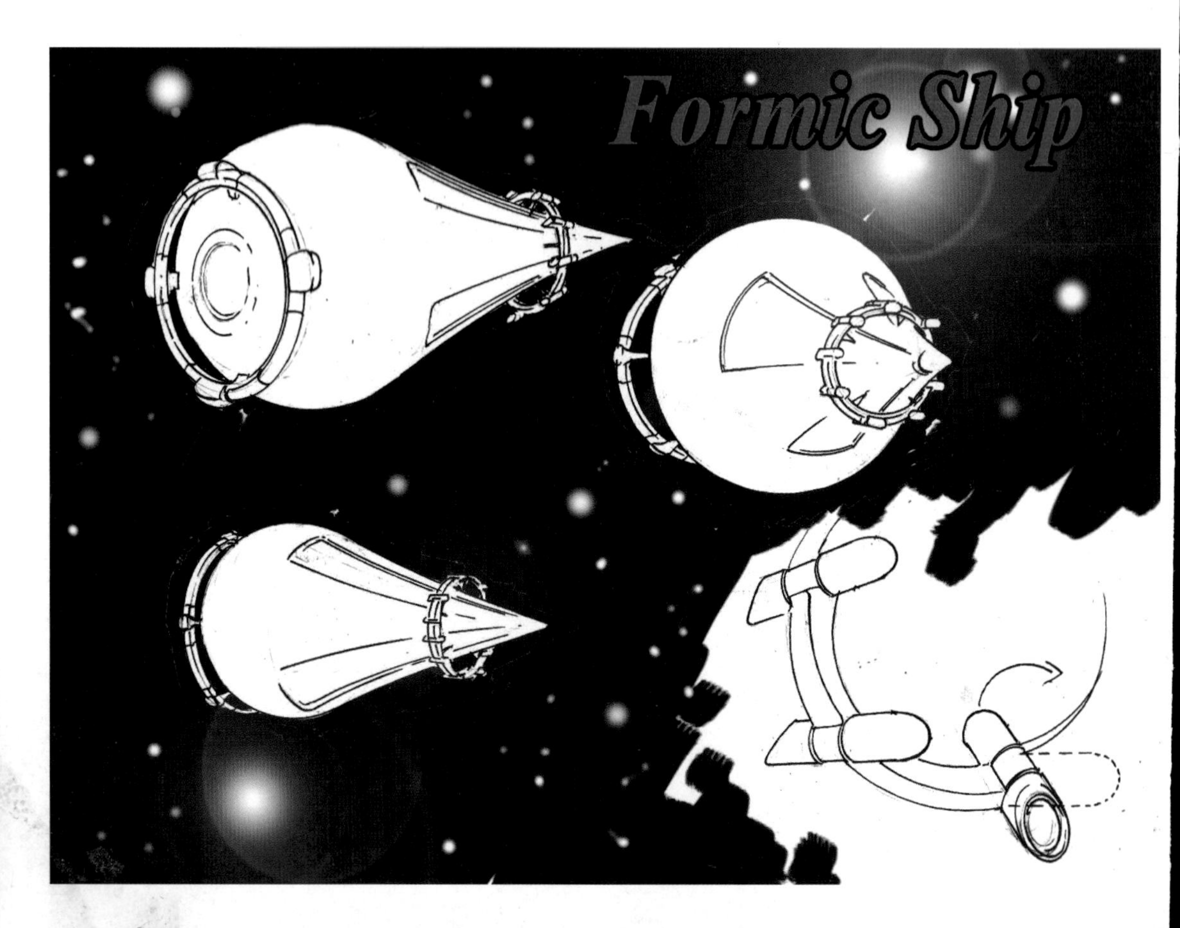
Formic Ship

EL CAVADOR --A

EL CAVADOR--B

EL CAVADOR--C

EL CAVADOR--D